, COMMA

The comma is used:

1. To separate independent clauses joined by a coordinate or correlative conjunction (as *and, but, for, nor,* and *or*): *It snowed yesterday, and today the road is closed.*

2. To separate independent clauses not joined by a conjunction when the clauses are short, closely related, and have no commas within: *I came, I saw, I conquered.*

3. After a dependent clause that precedes the main clause: *If there is any error, please let us know.*

4. To set off a nonrestrictive clause, phrase, or word: *Joan Smith, who lives next door, is ill.* (But *not* in the case of a restrictive clause as in: *The girl who lives next door is ill.*)

5. To set off parenthetical expressions, whether words, phrases, or clauses: *Our host, Bill Martin, is an excellent cook.*

6. To set off words or phrases expressing contrast: *Mr. Smith, not Mr. Jones, was elected.*

7. To set off transitional words and expressions (as *in short, of course*) or conjunctive adverbs (as *however, consequently, therefore*): *We found, in short, many errors in his work. Your question, however, remained unanswered.*

8. After expressions that introduce an example or illustration (as *namely, i.e., for example*): *Some of the presidential candidates, i.e., Smith, Jones, Brown, are also senators.*

10. To separate two words or figures that might otherwise be misunderstood: *To Mary, Louise was very kind. Instead of hundreds, thousands came.*

11. To separate two adjectives that modify the same noun and can be interchanged in position: *an eager, restless young man.* (But *not* in: *three silver spoons; a rare second chance.*)

12. To set off a short direct quotation: *He said, "Now or never."*

13. To set off a word or phrase in direct address: *Please go, Mary, I'm tired.*

14. To indicate the omission of a word or words: *Then we had much, now nothing.*

15. After a statement followed by a direct question: *You are sure, are you not?*

16. To set off items in dates, addresses, names of places: *She was born on June 5, 1936, at 64 Chestnut Street, Boston, Massachusetts.*

17. To separate a proper name from a title: *Philip Smith, Esq.*

18. After the salutation in informal correspondence: *Dear Mary,*

19. After the complimentary close of a letter: *Very truly yours,*

20. To separate an inverted name or phrase: *Jones, Edith.*

21. To separate thousands, millions, etc., in numbers of four or more digits: *5,256; 1,000,000.*

The
Word Book III

The Word Book III

BASED ON

THE AMERICAN HERITAGE DICTIONARY

compiled by
Kaethe Ellis

Houghton Mifflin Company · Boston

Editor for the revised edition, Beth Jaffe.

Library of Congress Cataloging-in-Publication Data

Ellis, Kaethe
   The Word book III : based on the American heritage dictionary / compiled by Kaethe Ellis.
     p.   cm.
   ISBN 0-395-53957-9
   1. English language—Pronunciation. 2. English language—Syllabication. I. American Heritage dictionary II. Title: Word book 3. III. Title: Word book three.
PE1146.E43   1990
428.1—dc20   90-4059
                                 CIP

Contents

How to Use This Book

The Word Book III presents basic information about the most commonly used words in the English language: how to spell a word, how to divide a word into syllables, and which syllables are stressed when a word is pronounced. The list of more than 40,000 words contained in this new edition is drawn from the files of *The American Heritage Dictionary: Second College Edition.* Word selection is based on the latest computer frequency studies developed by Houghton Mifflin Company, a leader in dictionary publishing and a pioneer in the creation of computer software for spelling verification and correction.

Obsolete, rare, and archaic forms have not been included in *The Word Book III.* Many colloquial words and technical and scientific terms, particularly those in common use, have been entered. Proper names and nouns have been omitted unless they appear as part of another, frequently used compound.

Normally, one-syllable words have not been entered, unless they present spelling difficulties, may be confused with another word, have irregular inflected forms, or do not appear elsewhere in the book as part of a compound form.

The Word Book III also has special features that will save you time and effort: a Guide to Plurals, showing how to form them; an explanation of the Seven Basic Rules of Spelling; and an alphabetical list of the most commonly used abbreviations.

Although *The Word Book III* is simple to use, the following guide will help you make the maximum utilization of its special benefits and features.

DIVISION OF WORDS

The Word Book III clearly shows how a word may be divided into syllables. Such divisions are indicated by a centered dot, by an accent mark, or by a hyphen:

ce•ment′   e•vap′o•ra′tion   top′sy-tur′vy

Note: Whenever a hyphen is indicated in an entry word, that hyphen is part of the word, and it must be retained when the word is used.

At the end of a line of type, a word may be broken wherever a syllable division is indicated. However, it is good English practice to observe these exceptions:

a. A syllable consisting of a single letter should not be separated from the rest of the word, as in:

a•bide′   stealth′y

(Many typesetters also consider it bad practice to separate initial or final syllables of two letters, such as the prefix *un-* or the suffix *-er*. If possible, it is better to avoid such divisions.)

b. A hyphenated word should be divided only at the hyphen.

A MATTER OF STRESS

The Word Book III indicates whenever a syllable is stressed in pronunciation. Two different stress marks are used. The first, a boldface stress, indicates the syllable that receives the primary stress in the word:

cen′ter   le′gal

Normally, only one syllable in a word receives primary stress. However, certain compound words may have more than one primary stress. *The Word Book III* will aid you in such cases.

The second mark, a lighter stress, indicates syllables that are not as strong as the one marked with a primary stress, but are still stronger than unmarked syllables:

def′i•ni′tion   re•gen′er•a′tion

At times, syllable stress depends on how a word is used; for example:

rec′ord (noun)   pre•fix′ (verb)

re•cord′ (verb)   pre′fix′ (noun)

The Word Book III indicates when such a shift in stress occurs; it also indicates whenever a plural form has an added stress or a shift in stress:

for′mu•la *pl.*
-las *or* -lae′

INFLECTED FORMS

In *The Word Book III* all irregular inflected forms have been included at the main entry for that word. These irregular inflected forms include noun plurals; the past tense, past participle, and present participle of verbs; and comparative and superlative forms of adjectives whenever the syllabic division of such a word changes. Such irregular forms—except, of course, in the case of one-syllable entries or forms—have been "clipped," or shortened, to save space:

ac′ti•vate′, -vat′ed,	ce′cum *pl.* -ca	swim, swam,
-vat′ing	fly, flew, flown,	swum, swim′ming
brave, brav′er,	fly′ing	wake, woke,
brav′est	po′di•um *pl.* -di•a	waked *or* woke
bring, brought,	*or* -di•ums	*or* wok′en,
bring′ing		wak′ing

In the above example, you will notice that verbs may have two or three added inflected forms. If only two forms are given, the first is both the past tense and the past participle (e.g., *brought*); if three forms are given, the first is the past tense, the second the past participle (e.g., *swam*—past tense; *swum*—past participle). If there are alternate forms for inflected forms, these are also shown (e.g., the alternate plurals -*dia* or -*diums* for *podium;* the alternate past participles *waked* or *woke* or *woken* or *wake*).

Note: Words chosen for inclusion in *The Word Book III* show the most complicated forms of that particular word. Consequently words such as *package* appear as a verb:

pack′age, -aged, -ag•ing

However, *package* is also a noun, and may be used as a modifier, or adjective. In such cases, *The Word Book III* includes only the part of speech that has irregular inflected forms, unless the stress pattern or word division changes.

WORDS LIKELY TO BE CONFUSED
OR MISUSED

In *The Word Book III*, glosses, or short identifying definitions, are given for all pairs or sets of words that are likely to be confused. If the words are separated alphabetically, cross-references to the other words are included.

Such words fall into three categories:

a. Homophones, or words that are pronounced the same but spelled differently:

yew *(tree)*	Yule *(Christmas)*
♦ *ewe, you*	♦ *you'll*

Note: many such sets of homophones are given, even though one of the words may not have a separate entry.

b. Words that are likely to be confused because they are closely related in spelling or pronunciation:

ac•cept *(to receive)*	a•dopt′ *(to choose)*
♦ *except*	♦ *adapt, adept*

c. Troublesome words whose meanings are likely to be misused:

bi•week′ly *(once* sem′i•week′ly
in two weeks) *(twice a week)*
 ♦ *semiweekly*   ♦ *biweekly*

Should such words fall in regular alphabetical order, only the gloss is shown:

co′co *(palm tree)* toil *(labor)*
co′coa *(beverage)* toile *(fabric)*

These glosses will help you quickly identify and locate the word you want. For further information on the usage of words, you should consult a dictionary.

VARIANTS

The Word Book III includes variant spellings of words whenever these different spellings are in common use in English. Such variant spellings appear only at the main entry for that word. If the variants are used almost equally, they appear as follows:

clay′ey *or* clay′ish

For most words, however, one form is preferred over the other:

out′size′ *also* o′ver•all′ *also*
out′sized′   o′ver•all′

As noted above in the section on inflected forms, all variant verb forms and plurals are also indicated.

PREFIXES

Many words that have prefixes like *self-* and *un-* have been included in *The Word Book III,* but it is impossible to include all such words. However, most prefixes follow regular rules when they are combined with other words. The following is a brief guide to the most commonly used prefixes.

Prefix	*Compounds are usually formed:*
anti- non- pre- pro- semi- un-	Without a hyphen, unless the prefix is followed by a capital letter.
out- over-	Without a hyphen.
re-	Without a hyphen, unless a distinction must be made between a word in which the prefix means "again" or "anew" and a word that has a special meaning: *re-creation* and *recreation*.
self-	With a hyphen.

A

aard′vark′
a•back′
ab′a•cus *pl.* -cus•es *or* -ci′
a•baft′
ab′a•lo′ne
a•ban′don
a•ban′doned
a•base′, a•based′, a•bas′ing
a•bash′
a•bate′, a•bat′ed, a•bat′ing
ab′at•toir′
ab′ba•cy *pl.* -cies
ab′bé
ab′bess
ab′bey *pl.* -beys
ab′bot
ab•bre′vi•ate′, -at′ed, -at′ing
ab•bre′vi•a′tion
ab•bre′vi•a′tor
ab′di•cate′, -cat′ed, -cat′ing
ab′di•ca′tion
ab′di•ca′tor
ab′do•men
ab•dom′i•nal
ab•duct′
ab•duc′tion
ab•duc′tor
a•beam′
a′be•ce•dar′i•an

a•bed′
ab•er′rant
ab•er•ra′tion
a•bet′, a•bet′ted, a•bet′ting
a•bet′tor *also* a•bet′ter
a•bey′ance
ab•hor′, -horred′, -hor′ring
ab•hor′rence
ab•hor′rent
a•bide′, a•bode′ *or* a•bid′ed, a•bid′ing
a•bil′i•ty
ab′ject′
ab•jec′tion
ab•jure′ *(to renounce),* -jured′, -jur′ing
♦*adjure*
ab•la′tion
ab′la•tive
a•blaze′
a′ble
a′ble-bod′ied
a•bloom′
ab•lu′tion
ab′ne•gate′, -gat′ed, -gat′ing
ab′ne•ga′tion
ab•nor′mal
ab′nor•mal′i•ty
a•board′
a•bode′
a•bol′ish
ab′o•li′tion

ab′o•li′tion•ar′y
ab′o•li′tion•ism
ab′o•li′tion•ist
A′-bomb′
a•bom′i•na•ble
a•bom′i•nate′, -nat′ed, -nat′ing
a•bom′i•na′tion
a•bom′i•na′tor
ab′o•rig′i•nal
ab′o•rig′i•ne′
a•bort′
a•bor′tion
a•bor′tion•ist
a•bor′tive
a•bound′
a•bout′
a•bout′-face′
a•bove′
a•bove′board′
a•bove′ground′
ab′ra•ca•dab′ra
a•brade′, a•brad′ed, a•brad′ing
a•bra′sion
a•bra′sive
a•breast′
a•bridge′, a•bridged′, a•bridg′ing
a•bridg′er
a•bridg′ment *also* a•bridge′ment
a•broad′
ab′ro•gate′, -gat′ed, -gat′ing
ab′ro•ga′tion
a•brupt′

ab'scess'
ab•scise', -scised',
  -scis'ing
ab•scis'sa pl. -sas or
  -sae
ab•scis'sion
ab•scond'
ab'sence
ab'sent
ab'sen•tee'
ab'sen•tee'ism
ab'sent-mind'ed
ab'sinthe
ab'so•lute'
ab'so•lute'ly
ab'so•lu'tion
ab'so•lut'ism
ab'so•lut'ist
ab'so•lu•tis'tic
ab•solv'a•ble
ab•solve', -solved',
  -solv'ing
ab•solv'er
ab•sorb' (to take in)
  ♦adsorb
ab•sorb'en•cy
ab•sorb'ent
ab•sorp'tion
ab•sorp'tive
ab•stain'
ab•ste'mi•ous
ab•sten'tion
ab'sti•nence
ab'sti•nent
ab•stract' adj.
ab'stract' n.
ab•stract' (to remove)

ab•stract' (to summa-
  rize)
ab•stract'ed
ab•strac'tion
ab•strac'tion•ism
ab•strac'tion•ist
ab•struse'
ab•surd'
ab•surd'ism
ab•surd'i•ty
a•bun'dance
a•bun'dant
a•buse', a•bused',
  a•bus'ing
a•bus'er
a•bu'sive
a•but', a•but'ted,
  a•but'ting
a•but'ment
a•but'ter
a•bysm'
a•bys'mal (unfathom-
  able, extreme)
  ♦abyssal
a•byss'
a•bys'sal (unfathom-
  able, of oceanic
  depths)
  ♦abysmal
a•ca'cia
ac'a•deme'
ac'a•de'mi•a
ac'a•dem'ic
ac'a•de•mi'cian
ac'a•dem'i•cism
  also a•cad'e•mism
a•cad'e•my

a•can'thus pl. -thus-
  es or -thi'
a' cap•pel'la
ac•cede' (to agree),
  -ced'ed, -ced'ing
  ♦exceed
ac•ced'ence
ac•ced'er
ac•cel'er•ant
ac•cel'er•ate', -at'ed,
  -at'ing
ac•cel'er•a'tion
ac•cel'er•a'tive
ac•cel'er•a'tor
ac•cel'er•om'e•ter
ac'cent'
ac•cen'tu•al
ac•cen'tu•ate', -at'-
  ed, -at'ing
ac•cen'tu•a'tion
ac•cept' (to receive)
  ♦except
ac•cept'a•bil'i•ty
ac•cept'a•ble
ac•cep'tance
ac'cep•ta'tion
ac'cess (entrance)
  ♦excess
ac•ces'si•bil'i•ty
ac•ces'si•ble
ac•ces'sion
ac•ces'so'ri•al
ac•ces'so•rize',
  -rized', -riz'ing
ac•ces'so•ry
ac'ci•dence
ac'ci•dent

ac'ci•den'tal
ac'ci•dent-prone'
ac•claim'
ac'cla•ma'tion
  (praise)
  ♦acclimation
ac•clam'a•to'ry
ac'cli•mate', -mat'ed,
  -mat'ing
ac'cli•ma'tion *(adap-
  tation)*
  ♦acclamation
ac•cli'ma•ti•za'tion
ac•cli'ma•tize',
  -tized', -tiz'ing
ac•cliv'i•ty
ac'co•lade'
ac•com'mo•date',
  -dat'ed, -dat'ing
ac•com'mo•da'tion
ac•com'mo•da'tive
ac•com'pa•ni•ment
ac•com'pa•nist
ac•com'pa•ny,
  -nied, -ny•ing
ac•com'plice
ac•com'plish
ac•com'plish•ment
ac•cord'
ac•cor'dance
ac•cord'ing•ly
ac•cor'di•on
ac•cor'di•on•ist
ac•cost'
ac•count'
ac•count'a•bil'i•ty
ac•count'a•ble

ac•count'ant
ac•count'ing
ac•cou'ter
ac•cou'ter•ment
ac•cred'it
ac•cred'i•ta'tion
ac•cre'tion
ac•cru'al
ac•crue', -crued',
  -cru'ing
ac•cul'tur•ate', -at'-
  ed, -at'ing
ac•cul'tur•a'tion
ac•cu'mu•late', -lat'-
  ed, -lat'ing
ac•cu'mu•la'tion
ac•cu'mu•la'tive
ac•cu'mu•la'tor
ac'cu•ra•cy
ac'cu•rate
ac•curs'ed *also* ac•
  curst'
ac•cu•sa'tion
ac•cu'sa•tive
ac•cu'sa•to'ri•al
ac•cuse', -cused',
  -cus'ing
ac•cus'er
ac•cus'tom
ace
a•cerb'
ac'er•bate', -bat'ed,
  -bat'ing
a•cer'bic
a•cer'bi•ty
ac'et•al'de•hyde'
ac'e•tate'

a•ce'tic *(of acetic
  acid)*
  ♦ascetic
ac'e•tone'
a•ce'tyl
a•cet'y•lene'
a•ce'tyl•sal'i•cyl'ic
  acid
ache, ached, ach'ing
a•chieve', a•chieved',
  a•chiev'ing
a•chieve'ment
a•chiev'er
A•chil'les
ach'ro•mat'ic
ac'id
a•cid'ic
a•cid'i•fi•ca'tion
a•cid'i•fy', -fied', -fy'-
  ing
a•cid'i•ty
ac'i•do'sis
a•cid'u•late', -lat'ed,
  -lat'ing
a•cid'u•la'tion
a•cid'u•lous
ac•knowl'edge,
  -edged, -edg•ing
ac•knowl'edge-
  a•ble
ac•knowl'edg•ment
  also ac•knowl'edge•
  ment
ac'me
ac'ne
ac'o•lyte'
ac'o•nite'

a'corn'
a•cous'tic *also*
 a•cous'ti•cal
a•cous'tics
ac•quaint'
ac•quain'tance
ac•quaint'ed
ac'qui•esce', -esced',
 -esc'ing
ac'qui•es'cence
ac'qui•es'cent
ac•quir'a•ble
ac•quire', -quired',
 -quir'ing
ac'qui•si'tion
ac•quis'i•tive
ac•quit', -quit'ted,
 -quit'ting
ac•quit'tal
ac•quit'tance
a'cre
a'cre•age
a'cre-foot'
ac'rid
a•crid'i•ty
ac'ri•mo'ni•ous
ac'ri•mo'ny
ac'ro•bat'
ac'ro•bat'ic
ac'ro•bat'ics
ac'ro•nym'
ac'ro•pho'bi•a
a•crop'o•lis
a•cross'
a•cross'-the-board'
a•cros'tic
a•cryl'ic acid

ACTH
ac'tin
act'ing
ac•tin'ic
ac'ti•nide'
ac•tin'i•um
ac'tion
ac'tion•a•ble
ac'ti•vate', -vat'ed,
 -vat'ing
ac'ti•va'tion
ac'ti•va'tor
ac'tive
ac'tiv•ism
ac'tiv•ist
ac•tiv'i•ty
ac'tor
ac'tress
ac'tu•al
ac'tu•al'i•ty
ac'tu•ar'y
ac'tu•ate', -at'ed, -at'-
 ing
ac'tu•a'tion
ac'tu•a'tor
a•cu'i•ty
a•cu'men
ac'u•punc'ture
a•cute'
ad *(advertisement)*
 ♦*add*
ad'age
a•da'gio *pl.* -gios
ad'a•mant
ad'a•man'tine'
a•dapt' *(to adjust)*
 ♦*adept, adopt*

a•dapt'a•bil'i•ty
a•dapt'a•ble
ad'ap•ta'tion
a•dapt'er *also* a•dap'-
 tor
a•dap'tive
add *(to total)*
 ♦*ad*
ad'dax'
ad'dend'
ad•den'dum *pl.* -da
add'er *(one that adds)*
ad'der *(snake)*
ad'der's-tongue'
ad•dict' *v.*
ad'dict *n.*
ad•dic'tion
ad•dic'tive
add'ing machine
ad•di'tion *(increase)*
 ♦*edition*
ad'di•tive
ad'dle, -dled, -dling
ad•dress'
ad•dress•ee'
ad•dress'er *also* ad-
 dres'sor
ad•duce', -duced',
 -duc'ing
ad•duct'
ad•duc'tion
ad'e•nine'
ad'e•noid'
ad'e•noi'dal
a•den'o•sine'
a•dept' *(skillful)*
 ♦*adapt, adopt*

ad′ept′ *(expert)*
ad′e•qua•cy
ad′e•quate
ad•here′ *(to stick),*
　-hered′, -her′ing
　♦*cohere*
ad•her′ence
ad•her′ent
ad•he′sion
ad•he′sive
ad hoc′
ad ho′mi•nem
ad′i•a•bat′ic
a•di′das® *also* A•di′-
　das
a•dieu′ *(good-by), pl.*
　a•dieus′ *or* a•dieux′
　♦*ado*
ad in•fi•ni•tum
a′di•os′
ad′i•pose′
ad•ja′cen•cy
ad•ja′cent
ad′jec•ti′val
ad′jec•tive
ad•join′
ad•join′ing
ad•journ′
ad•journ′ment
ad•judge′, -judged′,
　-judg′ing
ad•ju′di•cate′, -cat′-
　ed, -cat′ing
ad•ju′di•ca′tion
ad•ju′di•ca′tive
ad•ju′di•ca′tor
ad′junct′

ad•junc′tive
ad′ju•ra′tion
ad•jure′ *(to entreat),*
　-jured′, -jur′ing
　♦*abjure*
ad•just′
ad•just′a•ble
ad•just′er *also* ad-
　jus′tor
ad•just′ment
ad′ju•tant
ad-lib′, -libbed′, -lib′-
　bing
ad-lib′ber
ad′man′
ad•min′is•ter
ad•min′is•tra′tion
ad•min′is•tra′tive
ad•min′is•tra′tor
ad′mi•ra•ble
ad′mi•ral
ad′mi•ral•ty
ad′mi•ra′tion
ad•mire′, -mired′,
　-mir′ing
ad•mir′er
ad•mis′si•ble
ad•mis′sion
ad•mit′, -mit′ted,
　-mit′ting
ad•mit′tance
ad•mit′ted•ly
ad•mix′
ad•mix′ture
ad•mon′ish
ad•mon′ish•ment
ad′mo•ni′tion

ad•mon′i•to′ry
ad nau′se•am
a•do′ *(fuss)*
　♦*adieu*
a•do′be
ad′o•les′cence
ad′o•les′cent
A•don′is
a•dopt′ *(to take as*
　one's own)
　♦*adapt, adept*
a•dop′tion
a•dop′tive
a•dor′a•ble
ad′o•ra′tion
a•dore′, a•dored′,
　a•dor′ing
a•dor′er
a•dorn′
ad•re′nal
a•dren′a•line
ad•re′nal•ize′, -ized′,
　-iz′ing
a•drift′
a•droit′
ad•sorb′ *(to hold on a*
　surface)
　♦*absorb*
ad•sorp′tion
ad′u•late′, -lat′ed,
　-lat′ing
ad′u•la′tion
ad′u•la′tor
ad′u•la•to′ry
a•dult′
a•dul′ter•ant
a•dul′ter•ate′, -at′ed,

-at'ing
a·dul'ter·a'tion
a·dul'ter·er
a·dul'ter·ous
a·dul'ter·y
a·dult'hood'
ad·um'brate', -brat-
ed, -brat'ing
ad'um·bra'tion
ad·vance', -vanced',
-vanc'ing
ad·vance'ment
ad·vanc'er
ad·van'tage, -taged,
-tag·ing
ad'van·ta'geous
ad'vent
Ad·vent'ist
ad·ven·ti'tious
ad·ven'ture, -tured,
-tur·ing
ad·ven'tur·er
ad·ven'tur·ous
ad'verb'
ad·ver'bi·al
ad·ver·sar'y
ad·verse' (hostile, op-
posed)
♦averse
ad·ver'si·ty
ad·vert'
ad'ver·tise', -tised',
-tis'ing
ad'ver·tise'ment
ad'ver·tis'er
ad·vice' (guidance)
♦advise

ad·vis'a·bil'i·ty
ad·vis'a·ble
ad·vise' (to offer
counsel), -vised',
-vis'ing
♦advice
ad·vis'ed·ly
ad·vise'ment
ad·vis'er also ad·vi'-
sor
ad·vi'so·ry
ad'vo·ca·cy
ad'vo·cate', -cat'ed,
-cat'ing
adz or adze
ae'gis also e'gis
aer'ate', -at'ed, -at'ing
aer·a'tion
aer'a'tor
aer'i·al
aer'i·al·ist
aer'ie (nest)
♦airy, eerie
aer'o
aer'o·bat'ics
aer'obe'
aer·o'bic
aer·o'bi·cize',
-cized', -ciz'ing
aer·o'bics
aer'o·dy·nam'ics
aer·ol'o·gy
aer'o·me·chan'ics
aer'o·naut
aer'o·nau'tic also
aer'o·nau'ti·cal
aer'o·nau'tics

aer'o·pause'
aer'o·sol'
aer'o·space'
aer'o·stat'
aer'o·stat'ics
aes'thete' or es'thete'
aes·thet'ic or es·thet'-
ic
aes'the·ti'cian or es'-
the·ti'cian
aes·thet'i·cism or
es·thet'i·cism
aes·thet'ics or es-
thet'ics
aes'ti·vate', -vat'ed,
-vat'ing, also es'ti-
vate'
aes'ti·va'tion also es'-
ti·va'tion
a·far'
af'fa·bil'i·ty
af'fa·ble
af·fair'
af·fect' (to influence,
imitate)
♦effect
af'fec·ta'tion
af·fect'ed
af·fec'tion
af·fec'tion·ate
af·fec'tive
af·fect·less
af'fer·ent
af·fi'ance, -anced,
-anc·ing
af'fi·da·vit
af·fil'i·ate', -at'ed,

-at'ing
af·fil'i·a'tion
af·fin'i·ty
af·firm'
af·fir·ma'tion
af·fir'ma·tive
af·fix'
af·fla'tus
af·flict'
af·flic'tion
af'flu·ence
af'flu·ent
af·ford'
af·ford'a·ble
af·fray'
af·front'
Af'ghan' *(person, dog)*
af'ghan' *(blanket)*
a·fi'ci·o·na'do *pl.* -dos
a·field'
a·fire'
a·flame'
a·float'
a·flut'ter
a·foot'
a·fore'
a·fore'men'tioned
a·fore'said'
a·fore'thought'
a for'ti·o'ri
a·foul'
a·fraid'
a·fresh'
Af'ri·can
Af'ri·kaans'

Af'ri·kan'er
Af'ro' *pl.* -ros'
Af'ro-A·mer'i·can
aft
af'ter
af'ter·birth'
af'ter·burn'er
af'ter·care'
af'ter·deck'
af'ter·ef·fect'
af'ter·glow'
af'ter·im'age
af'ter·life'
af'ter·math'
af'ter·noon'
af'ter·taste'
af'ter·thought'
af'ter·ward *also* af'ter·wards
af'ter·world'
a·gain'
a·gainst'
a·gape'
a'gar *also* a'gar'-a'gar
ag'ate
a·ga've
age, aged, ag'ing
aged *(of the age of)*
a'ged *(elderly)*
age'ism'
age'less
age'-long'
a'gen·cy
a·gen'da
a·gen'dum *pl.* -da *or* -dums
a'gent

a'gent·ry
age'-old'
ag'er·a'tum
ag·glom'er·ate', -at'ed, -at'ing
ag·glom'er·a'tion
ag·glu'ti·nate', -nat'ed, -nat'ing
ag·glu'ti·na'tion
ag·glu'ti·na'tive
ag·glu'ti·nin
ag·gran'dize', -dized', -diz'ing
ag·gran'dize·ment
ag·gran'diz'er
ag'gra·vate', -vat'ed, -vat'ing
ag'gra·va'tion
ag'gra·va'tor
ag'gre·gate', -gat'ed, -gat'ing
ag'gre·ga'tion
ag'gre·ga'tor
ag·gres'sion
ag·gres'sive
ag·gres'sor
ag·grieve', -grieved', -griev'ing
a·ghast'
ag'ile
a·gil'i·ty
ag'i·tate', -tat'ed, -tat'ing
ag'i·ta'tion
ag'i·ta'tor
a·gleam'
a·gley'

a•glim′mer
a•glit′ter
a•glow′
ag•nos′tic
ag•nos′ti•cism
a•go′
a•gog′
a•gon′ic
ag′o•nize′, -nized′,
  -niz′ing
ag′o•ny
ag′o•ra pl. -rae′ or
  -ras
ag′o•ra•pho′bi•a
ag′o•ra•pho′bic
a•gou′ti pl. -tis or
  -ties
a•grar′i•an
a•grar′i•an•ism
a•gree′, a•greed′,
  a•gree′ing
a•gree′a•ble
a•gree′ment
ag′ri•busi′ness
ag′ri•cul′tur•al
ag′ri•cul′ture
ag′ri•cul′tur•ist
ag′ro•chem′i•cal
ag′ro•nom′ic also ag′-
  ro•nom′i•cal
a•gron′o•mist
a•gron′o•my
a•ground′
a′gue
a•head′
a•hoy′
aid (to help)

aide (assistant)
aide′-de-camp′ pl.
  aides′-de-camp′
ai•grette′ or ai•gret′
ail (to feel ill)
  ◆ale
ai•lan′thus
ai′le•ron′
ail′ing
ail′ment
aim′less
air (atmosphere)
  ◆are (metric unit),
  e′er, ere, heir
air′borne′
air′brush′
air′bus′
air′-con•di′tion v.
air′-cool′
air′craft′ pl. -craft
air′crew′
air′date′
air′drome′
air′drop′
Aire′dale′
air′field′
air′flow′
air′foil′
air′glow′
air′i•ness
air′less
air′lift′
air′line′
air′lin′er
air′mail′ v. & adj.
air′man
air′mo′bile

air′plane′
air′port′
air′pow′er
air′ship′
air′sick′
air′sick′ness
air′space′
air′strip′
air′tight′
air′-to-air′ missile
air′-to-sur′face
  missile
air′waves′
air′way′
air′wor′thy
air′y (breezy)
  ◆aerie
aisle (passageway)
  ◆I'll, isle
a•jar′
a•kim′bo
a•kin′
Al′a•bam′i•an also
  Al′a•bam′an
al′a•bas′ter
à′ la carte′
a•lac′ri•ty
A•lad′din
à′ la king′
à′ la mode′
a•larm′
a•larm′ist
a•las′
A•las′kan
alb
al′ba•core′
Al•ba′ni•an

al′ba•tross′
al•be′do *pl.* -dos
al•be′it
Al•ber′tan
al′bi•nism′
al•bi′no *pl.* -nos
al′bum
al•bu′men *(egg white)*
al•bu′min *(protein)*
al•caz′ar
al•chem′i•cal *or* al-chem′ic
al′che•mist
al′che•my
al′co•hol′
al′co•hol′ic
al′co•hol•ism
al′cove′
al′de•hyde′
al den′te
al′der
al′der•man
al′der•man•cy
ale *(beverage)*
   ♦*ail*
a•lee′
ale′house′
a•lem′bic
a•lert′
ale′wife′
a•lex′i•a
al•fal′fa
al•fres′co
al′gae *sing.* -ga
al′gal
al′ge•bra

al′ge•bra′ic
al′ge•bra′ist
Al•ge′ri•an
al′gid
AL′GOL′
al′go•rithm′
a′li•as
a′li•bi′ *pl.* -bis′
a′li•en
al′ien•a•ble
al′ien•ate′, -at′ed, -at′-ing
al′ien•a′tion
al′ien•a′tor
al′ien•ist
a•light′, a•light′ed *or* a•lit′, a•light′ing
a•lign′ *also* a•line′, a•lined′, a•lin′ing
a•lign′ment *also* a•line′ment
a•like′
al′i•ment
al′i•men′ta•ry
al′i•men•ta′tion
al′i•mo′ny
al′i•phat′ic
al′i•quant′
al′i•quot′
a•live′
al′ka•li′ *pl.* -lis′ *or* -lies′
al′ka•line′
al′ka•lin′i•ty
al′ka•li•za′tion
al′ka•lize′, -lized′, -liz′ing, *also* al′ka-

lin•ize′, -ized′, iz′ing
al′ka•loid′
al′ka•lo′sis
al′kyd
al′kyl
all *(total)*
   ♦*awl*
Al′lah
all′-A•mer′i•can
al•lan′to•is *pl.* -i•des
al•lay′
al′le•ga′tion
al•lege′, -leged′, -leg′-ing
al•leg′ed•ly
al•le′giance
al′le•gor′ic *also* al′le-gor′i•cal
al′le•go′rist
al′le•go′ry
al•le′gro *pl.* -gros
al•le′le
al•le′lic
al•le•lu′ia
al′le•mande′
al′ler•gen
al′ler•gen′ic
al•ler′gic
al′ler•gist
al′ler•gy
al•le′vi•ate′, -at′ed, -at′ing
al•le′vi•a′tion
al•le′vi•a′tor
al′ley *(passageway)*
   ♦*ally*
al′ley•way′

al·li'ance
al'lied'
al'li·ga'tor
all'-im·por'tant *adj.*
al·lit'er·ate', -at'ed,
　-at'ing
al·lit'er·a'tion
al·lit'er·a'tive
al·lo·cate', -cat'ed,
　-cat'ing
al·lo·ca'tion
al'lo·morph'
al'lo·mor'phic
al'lo·nym'
al'lo·path'ic
al·lop'a·thy
al'lo·phone'
al'lo·phon'ic
al·lot', -lot'ted, -lot'-
　ting
al·lot'ment
al'lo·trope'
al'lo·trop'ic *also* al'-
　lo·trop'i·cal
al·lot'ro·py
all'-out' *adj.*
all'-o'ver *adj.*
al·low'
al·low'a·ble
al·low'ance
al·low'ed·ly
al·loy' *n.*
al·loy' *v.*
all'-pur'pose *adj.*
all read'y *(completely*
　prepared)
　♦*already*

all right
all'-round' *adj., also*
　all'-a·round'
all'spice'
all'-star' *adj. & n.*
all'-time' *adj.*
all to·geth'er *(collec-*
　tively)
　♦*altogether*
al·lude' *(to refer to),*
　-lud'ed, -lud'ing
　♦*elude*
al·lure', -lured', -lur'-
　ing
al·lu'sion *(reference)*
　♦*illusion*
al·lu'sive *(suggestive)*
　♦*elusive, illusive*
al·lu'vi·al
al·lu'vi·um *pl.* -vi-
　ums *or* -vi·a
al·ly', -lied', -ly'ing
al'ly' *(friend)*
　♦*alley*
al'ma ma'ter *or* Al'-
　ma Ma'ter
al'ma·nac'
al·might'y
al'mond
al'mo·ner
al'most'
alms'giv'er
al·ni'co' *pl.* -cos'
al'oe
a·loft'
a·lo'ha'
a·lone'

a·long'
a·long'shore'
a·long'side'
a·loof'
a·loud' *(audibly)*
　♦*allowed*
al·pac'a
al'pen·horn'
al'pen·stock'
al'pha
al'pha·bet'
al'pha·bet'i·cal *also*
　al'pha·bet'ic
al'pha·bet·ize',
　-ized', -iz'ing
al'pha·nu·mer'ic
　also al'pha·mer'ic
al'pine' *(of high*
　mountains)
Al'pine' *(of the Alps)*
al·read'y *(previously)*
　♦*all ready*
al'so
al'so-ran'
al'tar *(religious table)*
　♦*alter*
al'tar·piece'
al'ter *(to change)*
　♦*altar*
al'ter·a'tion
al'ter·a'tive
al'ter·cate', -cat'ed,
　-cat'ing
al'ter·ca'tion
al'ter·nate *(happen-*
　ing in turn)
　♦*alternative*

al'ter•nate' *(to occur in turn),* -nat'ed, -nat'ing
al'ter•na'tion
al•ter'na•tive *(allowing a choice)*
♦alternate
al'ter•na'tor
al•the'a *also* al•thae'a
alt'horn'
al•though'
al•tim'e•ter
al'ti•tude'
al'ti•tu'di•nal
al'to *pl.* -tos
al'to•cu'mu•lus
al'to•geth'er *(completely)*
♦all together
al'to•stra'tus
al•tru'ism
al'tru•ist
al'tru•is'tic
al'um
a•lu'mi•na
a•lu'min•ize', -ized', -iz'ing
a•lu'mi•nous
a•lu'mi•num
a•lum'na *pl.* -nae'
a•lum'nus *pl.* -ni'
al•ve'o•lar
al•ve'o•lus *pl.* -li'
al'ways
a•lys'sum
a•main'
a•mal'gam

a•mal'ga•mate', -mat'ed, -mat'ing
a•mal'ga•ma'tion
a•mal'ga•ma'tor
am'a•ni'ta
a•man'u•en'sis *pl.* -ses
am'a•ranth'
am'a•ran'thine
am'a•ryl'lis
a•mass'
am'a•teur'
am'a•teur'ish
am'a•teur'ism
am'a•to'ry
a•maze', a•mazed', a•maz'ing
a•maze'ment
Am'a•zon' *also* am'a•zon
Am'a•zo'ni•an *also* am'a•zo'ni•an
am•bas'sa•dor
am•bas'sa•do'ri•al
am'ber
am'ber•gris'
am'bi•ance *also* am'bi•ence
am'bi•dex•ter'i•ty
am'bi•dex'trous
am'bi•ent
am'bi•gu'i•ty
am•big'u•ous
am•bi'tion
am•bi'tious
am•biv'a•lence
am•biv'a•lent

am'ble, -bled, -bling
am•bro'sia
am•bro'sial
am'bu•lance
am'bu•la•to'ry
am'bus•cade'
am'bush'
a•me'lio•rate', -rat'ed, -rat'ing
a•me'lio•ra'tion
a•me'lio•ra'tive
a•me'lio•ra'tor
a•men'
a•me'na•bil'i•ty
a•me'na•ble
a•mend *(to alter)*
♦emend
a•men'da•to'ry
a•mend'ment
a•mends'
a•men'i•ty
a•merce', a•merced', a•merc'ing
A•mer'i•can
A•mer'i•ca'na
A•mer'i•can•ism
A•mer'i•can•i•za'tion
A•mer'i•can•ize', -ized', -iz'ing
am'er•i'ci•um
am'e•thyst
a'mi•a•bil'i•ty
a'mi•a•ble
am'i•ca•bil'i•ty
am'i•ca•ble
am'ice

a•mid′ *also* a•midst′
am′ide′
a•mid′ships′
a•mi′go pl. -gos
a•mine′
a•mi′no acid
A′mish
a•miss′
a′mi•to′sis
a′mi•tot′ic
am′i•ty
am′me′ter
am′mo
am•mo′nia
am′mon•ite′
am•mo′ni•um
am′mu•ni′tion
am•ne′sia
am•ne′si•ac′
am′nes•ty
am•ni•o•cen•te′sis
  pl. -ses′
am′ni•on
a•moe′ba *or* a•me′ba
  pl. -bas *or* -bae
a•moe′bic *or* a•me′-
  bic
a•mong′ *also*
  a•mongst′
a•mon′til•la′do *pl.*
  -dos
a•mor′al
a′mo•ral′i•ty
am′o•rous
a•mor′phous
am′or•ti•za′tion
am′or•tize′, -tized′,

-tiz′ing
a•mount′
a•mour′
a•mour′-pro′pre
am′per•age
am′pere′
am′per•sand′
am•phet′a•mine′
am•phib′i•an
am•phib′i•ous
am′phi•bole′
am′phi•the′a•ter
am•pho•ra *pl.* -rae′
  or -ras
am′ple
am′pli•fi•ca′tion
am′pli•fi′er
am′pli•fy′, -fied′, -fy′-
  ing
am′pli•tude′
am′ply
am′poule *or* am′pule
am′pu•tate′, -tat′ed,
  -tat′ing
am′pu•ta′tion
am′pu•ta′tor
am′pu•tee′
Am′trak′
a•muck′ *also* a•mok′
am′u•let
a•muse′, a•mused′,
  a•mus′ing
a•muse′ment
am′yl
am′y•lase′
am′y•lop′sin
An′a•bap′tist

an′a•bol′ic
a•nab′o•lism′
a•nach′ro•nism′
a•nach′ro•nis′tic
an•a•con′da
an′aer•obe′
an′aer•o′bic
an′a•gram′
a′nal
an′al•ge′si•a
an′al•ge′sic
an′a•log′ computer
a•nal′o•gous
an′a•logue′ *also* an′-
  a•log′
a•nal′o•gy
a•nal′y•sis *pl.* -ses′
an′a•lyst *(one who
  analyzes)*
  ♦*annalist*
an′a•lyt′ic *also* an′-
  a•lyt′i•cal
an′a•lyze′, -lyzed′,
  -lyz′ing
an′a•pest′ *also* an′-
  a•paest′
an′a•phase′
an′a•phy•lac′tic
an′a•phy•lax′is
an•ar′chic *or* an•ar′-
  chi•cal
an′ar•chism
an′ar•chist
an′ar•chis′tic
an′ar•chy
an•as′tig•mat′ic
a•nath′e•ma *pl.* -mas

a•nath'e•ma•tize',
-tized', -tiz'ing
an'a•tom'i•cal *also*
an'a•tom'ic
a•nat'o•mist
a•nat'o•mize',
-mized', -miz'ing
a•nat'o•my
an'ces'tor
an•ces'tral
an'ces'try
an'chor
an'chor•age
an'cho•rite'
an'cho•rit'ic
an'chor•man'
an'chor•wom'an
an'cho'vy
an'cient
an'cil•lar'y
an•dan'te
an•dan•ti'no *pl.* -nos
and'i'ron
and/or
an'dro•gen
an'dro•gen'ic
an•drog'y•nous
an•drog'y•ny
an'droid'
an'ec•do'tal
an'ec•dote'
a•ne'mi•a *also*
a•nae'mi•a
a•ne'mic *also* a•nae'-
mic
an'e•mom'e•ter
a•nem'o•ne

a•nent'
an'er•oid'
barometer
an'es•the'sia *also* an'-
aes•the'sia
an'es•the'si•ol'-
o•gist *also* an'aes-
the'si•ol'o•gist
an'es•the'si•ol'o•gy
also an'aes•the'si•ol'-
o•gy
an'es•thet'ic *also* an'-
aes•thet'ic
an•es'the•tist *also*
an•aes'the•tist
an•es'the•ti•za'tion
also an•aes'the•ti•
za'tion
an•es'the•tize',
-tized', -tiz'ing, *also*
an•aes'the•tize'
an'eu•rysm *also* an'-
eu•rism
a•new'
an'gel
an'gel•fish' *pl.* -fish'
or -fish'es
an•gel'ic *also* an•gel'-
i•cal
an•gel'i•ca
an'ger
an•gi'na pec'to•ris
an'gi•o•sperm'
an'gle, -gled, -gling
an'gler
an'gler•fish' *pl.* -fish'
or -fish'es

an'gle•worm'
An'gli•can
An'gli•can•ism
An'gli•cism
An'gli•ci•za'tion
An'gli•cize', -cized',
-ciz'ing
an'gling
An'glo-A•mer'i•can
An'glo•phile'
An'glo•phil'ic
An'glo•phobe'
An'glo•pho'bic
An'glo•phone'
An'glo-Sax'on
an•go'ra *(yarn)*
An•go'ra *(cat, goat,*
rabbit)
an'gos•tu'ra
an'gry
angst
ang'strom *or* ång'-
ström
an'guish
an'gu•lar
an'gu•lar'i•ty
an•hy'dride'
an•hy'drite'
an•hy'drous
an'i•line *also* an'i•lin
an'i•mad•ver'sion
an'i•mad•vert'
an'i•mal
an'i•mal'cule
an'i•mal•ism
an'i•mal•is'tic
an'i•mate', -mat'ed,

-mat′ing
an′i•ma′tion
an′i•ma′tor *also* an′-i•mat′er
an′i•mism
an′i•mist
an′i•mis′tic
an′i•mos′i•ty
an′i•mus
an′i′on
an′i•on′ic
an′ise
an′i•seed′
an′i•sette′
an′kle
an′kle•bone′
an′klet
an′nal•ist *(chronicler)*
  ♦*analyst*
an′nals
an•neal′
an′ne•lid
an•nex′ *v.*
an′nex′ *n.*
an′nex•a′tion
an•ni′hi•late′, -lat′-ed, -lat′ing
an•ni′hi•la′tion
an•ni′hi•la′tive
an•ni′hi•la′tor
an′ni•ver′sa•ry
an′no Dom′i•ni′
an′no•tate′, -tat′ed, -tat′ing
an′no•ta′tion
an′no•ta′tive
an′no•ta′tor

an•nounce′, -nounced′, -nounc′-ing
an•nounce′ment
an•nounc′er
an•noy′
an•noy′ance
an′nu•al
an′nu•al•ize′, -ized′, -iz′ing
an•nu′i•tant
an•nu′i•ty
an•nul′, -nulled′, -nul′ling
an′nu•lar
an•nul′ment
an′nu•lus *pl.* -lus•es *or* -li′
an•nun′ci•ate′, -at-ed, -at′ing
an•nun′ci•a′tion
an•nun′ci•a′tor
an′ode′
an′o•dize′, -dized′, -diz′ing
an′o•dyne′
a•noint′
a•noint′ment
a•nom′a•lous
a•nom′a•ly
a•nom′ic
an′o•mie *or* an′o•my
a•non′
an′o•nym′i•ty
a•non′y•mous
a•noph′e•les′
an′o•rec′tic *or* an′-

o•ret′ic, *also* an′-o•rex′ic
an′o•rex′ia nerv-o′sa
an•oth′er
an•ox′i•a
an•ox′ic
an′swer
an′swer•a•ble
an′swer•back′
ant *(insect)*
  ♦*aunt*
ant•ac′id
an•tag′o•nism
an•tag′o•nist
an•tag′o•nis′tic
an•tag′o•nize′, -nized′, -niz′ing
Ant•arc′tic
an′te, -ted *or* -teed, -te•ing
ant′eat′er
an′te-bel′lum
an′te•ce′dence
an′te•ce′dent
an′te•cham′ber
an′te•date′, -dat′ed, -dat′ing
an′te-di•lu′vi•an
an′te•lope′ *pl.* -lope *or* -lopes′
an′te me•rid′i•em
an•ten′na *pl.* -nae *or* -nas
an′te•pe′nult
an′te•pe•nul′ti-mate

an•te'ri•or
an'te•room'
an'them
an'ther
ant'hill'
an•thol'o•gist
an•thol'o•gize',
  -gized', -giz'ing
an•thol'o•gy
an'tho•zo'an
an'thra•cene'
an'thra•cite'
an'thrax'
an'thro•po•cen'tric
an'thro•poid'
an'thro•po•log'ic
  also an'thro•po•log'-
  i•cal
an'thro•pol'o•gist
an'thro•pol'o•gy
an'thro•po•mor'-
  phic
an'thro•po•mor'-
  phism
an'ti' pl. -tis'
an'ti•a•bor'tion
an'ti•air'craft'
an'ti•bal•lis'tic
  missile
an'ti•bi•o'sis
an'ti•bi•ot'ic
an'ti•bod'y
an'tic
an'ti•christ'
an•tic'i•pate', -pat'-
  ed, -pat'ing
an•tic'i•pa'tion

an•tic'i•pa'tor
an•tic'i•pa•to'ry
an'ti•cler'i•cal
an'ti•cli•mac'tic
an'ti•cli'max
an'ti•cline'
an'ti•co•ag'u•lant
an'ti•cy'clone
an'ti•de•pres'sant
an'ti•dot'al
an'ti•dote'
an'ti•freeze'
an'ti•gen also an'ti-
  gene
an'ti•gen'ic
an'ti-he'ro pl. -roes
an'ti•his'ta•mine'
an'ti•knock'
an'ti•log'a•rithm'
an'ti•ma•cas'sar
an'ti•mag•net'ic
an'ti•mat'ter
an'ti•mis'sile
  missile
an'ti•mo'ny
an'ti•neu•tri'no pl.
  -nos
an'ti•neu'tron
an'ti•ox'i•dant
an'ti•par'ti•cle
an'ti•pas'to pl. -tos
an'tip•a•thet'ic also
  an'tip•a•thet'i•cal
an•tip'a•thy
an'ti•per'son•nel'
an'ti•per'spi•rant
an'ti•phon'

an•tiph•o'nal
an•tiph'o•ny
an•tip'o•dal
an•tip'o•de'
an'ti•pode'
an•tip'o•des'
an'ti•pov'er•ty
an'ti•pro'ton
an'ti•py•ret'ic
an'ti•quar'i•an
an'ti•quar'y
an'ti•quate', -quat'-
  ed, -quat'ing
an'ti•qua'tion
an•tique', -tiqued',
  -tiqu'ing
an•tiq'ui•ty
an'ti-Sem'ite'
an'ti-Se•mit'ic
an'ti-Sem'i•tism
an'ti•sep'sis
an'ti•sep'tic
an'ti•slav'er•y
an'ti•smog'
an'ti•so'cial
an'ti•spas•mod'ic
an'ti•sub'ma•rine'
an'ti•take'o'ver
an'ti•tank'
an•tith'e•sis pl. -ses'
an'ti•thet'i•cal also
  an'ti•thet'ic
an'ti•tox'ic
an'ti•tox'in
an'ti•trades'
an'ti•trust'
an'ti•ven'in
ant'ler

ant'lered
an'to•nym'
an•ton'y•mous
ant'sy
a'nus *pl.* a'nus•es
an'vil
anx•i'e•ty
anx'ious
an'y
an'y•bod'y
an'y•how'
an'y•more'
an'y•one'
an'y•place'
an'y•thing'
an'y•time'
an'y•way'
an'y•where'
an'y•wise'
A'-O•K' *also*
  A'-O•kay' *adj. & adv.*
A'-one'
a•or'ta *pl.* -tas *or* -tae'
a•or'tal *or* a•or'tic
a'ou•dad'
a•pace'
a•part'
a•part'heid'
a•part'ment
ap'a•thet'ic
ap'a•thy
ape, aped, ap'ing
a•pé'ri•tif'
ap'er•ture'
a'pex' *pl.* a'pex'es *or*
  a'pi•ces'
a•pha'sia

a•pha'si•ac'
a•pha'sic
a•phe'li•on *pl.* -li•a
a'phid
aph'o•rism
aph'o•ris'tic
aph'ro•dis'i•ac
a'pi•a•rist
a'pi•ar'y
ap'i•cal
a'pi•cul'ture
a•piece'
ap'ish
a•plomb'
a•poc'a•lypse'
a•poc'a•lyp'tic *also*
  a•poc'a•lyp'ti•cal
A•poc'ry•pha
a•poc'ry•phal
ap'o•gee
a'po•lit'i•cal
A•pol'lo
a•pol'o•get'ic
ap'o•lo'gi•a
a•pol'o•gist
a•pol'o•gize',
  -gized', -giz'ing
a•pol'o•giz'er
a•pol'o•gy
ap'o•plec'tic
ap'o•plex'y
a•pos'ta•sy
a•pos'tate'
a pos•te'ri•o'ri
a•pos'tle
ap'os•tol'ic
a•pos'tro•phe

a•pos'tro•phize',
  -phized', -phiz'ing
a•poth'e•car'ies'
  measure
a•poth'e•car'y
ap'o•thegm' *(maxim)*
ap'o•them' *(geomet-*
  ric distance)
a•poth'e•o'sis *pl.*
  -ses'
Ap'pa•la'chi•an
ap•pall'
ap'pa•loo'sa
ap'pa•nage *also* ap'-
  a•nage
ap'pa•ra'tus *pl.* -tus
  or -tus•es
ap•par'el, -eled *or*
  -elled, -el'ing *or*
  -elling
ap•par'ent
ap'pa•ri'tion
ap•peal'
ap•pear'
ap•pear'ance
ap•pease', -peased',
  -peas'ing
ap•pease'ment
ap•peas'er
ap•pel'lant
ap•pel'late
ap'pel•la'tion
ap'pel•lee'
ap•pend'
ap•pend'age
ap'pen•dec'to•my
ap•pen•di•ci'tis

ap•pen'dix *pl.* -dix-
  es *or* -di•ces'
ap'per•ceive',
  -ceived', -ceiv'ing
ap'per•cep'tion
ap'per•tain'
ap•pe•tite'
ap'pe•tiz'er
ap'pe•tiz'ing
ap•plaud'
ap•plause'
ap'ple
ap'ple•jack'
ap'ple•sauce'
ap•pli'ance
ap'pli•ca•bil'i•ty
ap•pli•ca•ble
ap'pli•cant
ap'pli•ca'tion
ap'pli•ca'tor
ap•plied'
ap'pli•qué', -quéd',
  -qué'ing
ap•ply', -plied', -ply'-
  ing
ap•point'
ap•point'ee'
ap•point'ive
ap•point'ment
ap•por'tion
ap•por'tion•ment
ap•pose' *(to arrange
  side by side),*
  -posed', -pos'ing
  ♦*oppose*
ap'po•site *(appropri-
  ate)*

♦*opposite*
ap'po•si'tion
ap•pos'i•tive
ap•prais'al
ap•praise' *(to evalu-
  ate),* -praised',
  -prais'ing
  ♦*apprise*
ap•prais'er
ap•pre'cia•ble
ap•pre'ci•ate', -at'-
  ed, -at'ing
ap•pre'ci•a'tion
ap•pre'cia•tive
ap•pre'ci•a'tor
ap•pre•hend'
ap'pre•hen'sion
ap'pre•hen'sive
ap•pren'tice, -ticed,
  -tic•ing
ap•pren'tice•ship'
ap•prise' *(to inform),*
  -prised', -pris'ing
  ♦*appraise*
ap•proach'
ap•proach'a•bil'i•ty
ap•proach'a•ble
ap'pro•ba'tion
ap•pro'pri•ate', -at'-
  ed, -at'ing
ap•pro'pri•a'tion
ap•pro'pri•a'tor
ap•prov'al
ap•prove', -proved',
  -prov'ing
ap•prox'i•mate',
  -mat'ed, -mat'ing

ap•prox'i•ma'tion
ap•pur'te•nance
a'pri•cot'
A'pril
a pri•o'ri
a'pron
ap'ro•pos'
apse
ap'ti•tude'
apt'ly
aq'ua
aq'ua•ma•rine'
aq'ua•naut'
aq'ua•plane',
  -planed', -plan'ing
a•quar'i•um *pl.*
  -i•ums *or* -i•a
A•quar'i•us
a•quat'ic
aq'ua•tint'
aq'ue•duct'
a'que•ous
aq'ui•fer
aq'ui•line'
Ar'ab
ar'a•besque'
A•ra'bi•an
Ar'a•bic
ar'a•ble
a•rach'nid
a•rag'o•nite'
Ar'au•ca'ni•an
ar'bi•ter
ar'bi•trage'
ar'bi•tra•geur'
ar•bit'ra•ment
ar'bi•trar'y

ar′bi•trate′, -trat′ed,
-trat′ing
ar′bi•tra′tion
ar′bi•tra′tor
ar′bor
ar•bo′re•al
ar′bo•re′tum *pl.*
-tums *or* -ta
ar′bor•vi′tae
ar•bu′tus *pl.* -tus•es
arc *(to curve)*, arced *or*
arcked, arc′ing *or*
arck′ing
♦*ark*
ar•cade′
ar•cane′
arch
ar′chae•o•log′i•cal
or ar′chae•o•log′ic,
also ar′che•o•log′-
i•cal *or* ar′che•
o•log′ic
ar′chae•ol′o•gist *or*
ar′che•ol′o•gist
ar′chae•ol′o•gy *or*
ar′che•ol′o•gy
ar′chae•op′ter•yx
ar•cha′ic
ar′cha•ism
ar′cha•is′tic
arch′an′gel
arch•bish′op
arch•dea′con
arch•di•oc′e•san
arch•di′o•cese
arch•du′cal
arch•duch′ess

arch•duke′
arch•en′e•my
arch′er
arch′er•y
ar′che•typ′al *also* ar′-
che•typ′ic, ar′che-
typ′i•cal
ar′che•type′
arch•fiend′
ar′chi•e•pis′co•pal
ar′chi•pel′a•go′ *pl.*
-goes′ *or* -gos′
ar′chi•tect′
ar′chi•tec•ton′ic
also ar′chi•tec•ton′-
i•cal
ar′chi•tec•ton′ics
ar′chi•tec•tur′al
ar′chi•tec′ture
ar′chi•trave′
ar′chives′
ar′chi•vist
arch′ly
arch′way′
arc′tic
ar′den•cy
ar′dent
ar′dor
ar′du•ous
are *(metric unit)*
♦*air, e′er, ere, heir*
are *v.*
ar′e•a *(space)*
♦*aria*
Area Code *also* area
code
ar′e•a•way′

a•re′na
aren′t
Ar′es
ar′gent
Ar′gen•tine′ *also* Ar-
gen•tin′e•an
ar′gon′
ar′go•sy
ar′got
ar′gu•a•ble
ar′gue, -gued, -gu•ing
ar′gu•ment
ar′gu•men•ta′tion
ar′gu•men′ta•tive
ar′gyle′ *also* ar′gyll′
a′ri•a *(melody)*
♦*area*
ar′id
a•rid′i•ty
Ar′ies
a′right′
ar′il
a•rise′, a•rose′, a•ris-
en, a•ris′ing
ar′is•toc′ra•cy
a•ris′to•crat′
a•ris′to•crat′ic
Ar′is•to•te′li•an
also Ar′is•to•te′le-
an
a•rith′me•tic *n.*
ar′ith•met′ic *adj.,*
also ar′ith•met′i•cal
Ar′i•zo′nan
ark *(boat)*
♦*arc*
Ar•kan′san

ar•ma′da
ar′ma•dil′lo *pl.* -los
ar′ma•ment
ar′ma•ture′
arm′band′
arm′chair′
arm′ful′ *pl.* -fuls′
arm′hole′
ar′mi•stice
arm′let
arm′load′
ar•moire′
ar′mor
ar′mored
ar•mo′ri•al
ar′mor•y
arm′pit′
arm′rest′
arms
ar′my
ar′ni•ca
a•ro′ma
ar′o•mat′ic
a•round′
a•rouse′, a•roused′,
    a•rous′ing
ar•peg′gi•o *pl.* -os′
ar•raign′
ar•raign′ment
ar•range′, -ranged′,
    -rang′ing
ar•range′ment
ar•rang′er
ar′rant
ar′ras
ar•ray′
ar•rears′

ar•rest′
ar•rest•ee′
ar•ri′val
ar•rive′, -rived′, -riv′-
    ing
ar′ro•gance
ar′ro•gant
ar′ro•gate′, -gat′ed,
    -gat′ing
ar′ro•ga′tion
ar′ro•ga′tive
ar′ro•ga′tor
ar′row
ar′row•head′
ar′row•root′
ar•roy′o *pl.* -os
ar′se•nal
ar′se•nate
ar′se•nic
ar′son
ar′son•ist
art′ dec′o
ar•te′ri•al
ar•te′ri•ole′
ar•te′ri•o•scle•ro′-
    sis
ar•te′ri•o•scle•rot′-
    ic
ar′ter•y
ar•te′sian well
art′ful
ar•thrit′ic
ar•thri′tis
ar′thro•pod′
ar′ti•choke′
ar′ti•cle
ar•tic′u•lar

ar•tic′u•late′, -lat′ed,
    -lat′ing
ar•tic′u•la′tion
ar•tic′u•la′tor
ar′ti•fact′ *also* ar′te-
    fact′
ar′ti•fice
ar′ti•fi′cial
ar′ti•fi′ci•al′i•ty
ar•til′ler•y
ar′ti•san
art′ist
ar•tis′tic
art′ist•ry
art′less
art′ nou•veau′
art′work′
art′y
a•ru′gu•la
ar′um
as′a•fet′i•da
as•bes′tos *also* as-
    bes′tus
as•cend′
as•cen′dan•cy *also*
    as•cen′den•cy, as-
    cen′dance, as•cen′
    dence
as•cen′dant *also* as-
    cen′dent
as•cen′sion
as•cent′ *(upward
    slope)*
    ♦*assent*
as′cer•tain′
as•cet′ic *(austere)*
    ♦*acetic*

as•cet'i•cism
a•scor'bate
a•scor'bic acid
as'cot
as•cribe', -cribed', -crib'ing
as•crip'tion
a•sep'sis
a•sep'tic
a•sex'u•al
a•shamed'
ash'en
a•shore'
ash'tray'
A'sian
A'si•at'ic
a•side'
as'i•nine'
as'i•nin'i•ty
ask
a•skance'
a•skew'
a•slant'
a•sleep'
a•so'cial
asp
as•par'a•gus
as'pect'
as'pen
as•per'i•ty
as•perse', -persed', -pers'ing
as•per'sion
as'phalt'
as'pho•del'
as•phyx'i•a
as•phyx'i•ate', -at'ed, -at'ing
as•phyx'i•a'tion
as•phyx'i•a'tor
as'pic
as•pi•dis'tra
as'pi•rant
as•pi•rate', -rat'ed, -rat'ing
as'pi•ra'tion
as'pi•ra'tor
as•pire', -pired', -pir'ing
as'pi•rin
as'sa•gai' or as'se•gai
as•sail'
as•sail'a•ble
as•sail'ant
as•sas'sin
as•sas'si•nate', -nat'ed, -nat'ing
as•sas'si•na'tion
as•sault'
as'say' n.
as•say' (to analyze)
♦essay
as•sem'blage
as•sem'ble, -bled, -bling
as•sem'bly
as•sent' (agreement)
♦ascent
as•sert'
as•ser'tion
as•ser'tive
as•sess'
as•sess'a•ble
as•sess'ment
as•ses'sor
as'set'
as•sev'er•ate', -at'ed, -at'ing
as•si•du'i•ty
as•sid'u•ous
as•sign'
as•sig•na'tion
as•sign•ee'
as•sign'ment
as•sim'i•la•ble
as•sim'i•late', -lat'ed, -lat'ing
as•sim'i•la'tion
as•sim'i•la'tive also as•sim'i•la•to'ry
as•sist'
as•sis'tance
as•sis'tant
as•size'
as•so'ci•ate', -at'ed, -at'ing
as•so'ci•a'tion
as•so'ci•a'tive
as'so•nance
as'so•nant
as•sort'
as•sort'ed
as•sort'ment
as•suage', -suaged', -suag'ing
as•sume' (to take on), -sumed', -sum'ing
♦presume
as•sump'tion
as•sur'ance
as•sure' (to declare,

*make secure or cer-
tain),* -sured', -sur'-
ing
♦*ensure, insure*
as•sur•ed•ly
as'ta•tine'
as'ter
as'ter•isk'
as'ter•ism
a•stern'
as'ter•oid'
asth'ma
asth•mat'ic
as'tig•mat'ic
a•stig'ma•tism
a•stir'
a•ston'ish
a•ston'ish•ment
a•stound'
a•strad'dle
as'tra•khan'
as'tral
a•stray'
a•stride'
as•trin'gen•cy
as•trin'gent
as'tro•dome'
as'tro•labe'
as•trol'o•ger
as'tro•log'ic *also* as'-
tro•log'i•cal
as•trol'o•gy
as'tro•naut'
as'tro•nau'tic *also*
as'tro•nau'ti•cal
as'tro•nau'tics

as•tron'o•mer
as'tro•nom'i•cal
also as'tro•nom•ic
as•tron'o•my
as'tro•phys'i•cal
as'tro•phys'i•cist
as'tro•phys'ics
As'tro•Turf' ®
as•tute'
a•sun'der
a•sy'lum
a'sym•met'ric *also*
a'sym•met'ri•cal
a•sym'me•try
as'ymp•tote'
as'ymp•tot'ic *also*
as'ymp•tot'i•cal
a•syn'chro•nous
at'a•rac'tic *also* at'-
a•rax'ic
at'a•vism
at'a•vis'tic
a•tax'i•a *also* a•tax'y
a•tax'ic
at'el•ier'
a'the•ism
a'the•ist
a'the•is'tic *also*
a'the•is'ti•cal
ath'e•nae'um *also*
ath'e•ne'um
A•the'ni•an
a'the•o•ret'i•cal
a•thirst'
ath'lete'
ath'lete's foot'
ath•let'ic

ath•let'ics
a•thwart'
a•tilt'
At•lan'tic
At•lan'tis
at'las *(maps)*
At'las *(giant, missile)*
at'mos•phere'
at'mos•pher'ic *also*
at'mos•pher'i•cal
at'mos•pher'ics
a•toll'
at'om
a•tom'ic
at'om•i•za'tion
at'om•ize', -ized', -iz'-
ing
at'om•iz'er
a•to'nal
a'to•nal'i•ty
a•tone', a•toned',
a•ton'ing
a•tone'ment
a•top'
a•trem'ble
a•tri•um *pl.* a'tri•a *or*
a'tri•ums
a•tro'cious
a•troc'i•ty
a•troph'ic
at'ro•phy, -phied,
-phy•ing
at'ro•pine' *also* at'-
ro•pin
at•tach'
at'ta•ché'
at•tach'ment

at•tack′
at•tain′
at•tain′a•ble
at•tain′der
at•tain′ment
at•taint′
at′tar
at•tempt′
at•tend′
at•ten′dance
at•ten′dant
at•tend•ee′
at•ten′tion
at•ten′tive
at•ten′u•ate′, -at′ed,
  -at′ing
at•test′
at′tic
at•tire′, -tired′, -tir-
  ing
at′ti•tude′
at′ti•tu′di•nal
at′ti•tu′di•nize′,
  -nized′, -niz′ing
at•tor′ney pl. -neys
attorney general pl.
  attorneys general
at•tract′
at•trac′tion
at•trac′tive
at•trac′tor or at-
  tract′er
at•trib′ut•a•ble
at•trib′ute, -ut•ed,
  -ut•ing
at′tri•bute′ n.
at′tri•bu′tion

at•trib′u•tive
at•tri′tion
at•tune′, -tuned′,
  -tun′ing
a•twit′ter
a•typ′i•cal
au′burn
au cou•rant′
auc′tion
auc′tion•eer′
auc•to′ri•al
au•da′cious
au•dac′i•ty
au′di•al
au′di•bil′i•ty
au′di•ble
au′di•ence
au′di•o′ pl. -os′
au′di•o•cas•sette′
au′di•om′e•ter
au′di•o•phile′
au′di•o•tape′,
  -taped′, -tap′ing
au′di•o-vis′u•al adj.
au′di•o•vis′u•als n.
au′dit
au•di′tion
au′di•tor
au′di•to′ri•um pl.
  -ri•ums or -ri•a
au′di•to′ry
auf Wie′der•seh′en
au′ger (tool)
  ♦augur
aught (all, at all), also
  ought
aught (zero), also

ought
aug•ment′
aug′men•ta′tion
aug•men′ta•tive
au gra′tin
au′gur (to predict)
  ♦auger
au′gu•ry
au•gust′ (majestic)
Au′gust (month)
auk
auld lang syne′
aunt (relative)
  ♦ant
au′ra pl. -ras or rae
au′ral (of the ear)
  ♦oral
au′re•ate
au′re•ole′ also au•re′-
  o•la
au re•voir′
au′ri•cle (ear part)
  ♦oracle
au•ric′u•lar
au•rif′er•ous
au′rochs′
au•ro′ra
aurora aus•tra′lis
aurora bo•re•al′is
aus•cul•ta′tion
aus′pice pl. -pi•ces′
aus•pi′cious
aus•tere′
aus•ter′i•ty
aus′tral
Aus•tra′lian
aus•tra•lo•pith′-

e•cine′
Aus′tri•an
au′tarch′
au•teur′
au•teur′ism
au•then′tic
au•then′ti•cate′,
  -cat′ed, -cat′ing
au•then′ti•ca′tion
au•then′ti•ca′tor
au′then•tic′i•ty
au′thor
au•thor′i•tar′i•an
au•thor′i•tar′i•an-
  ism
au•thor′i•ta′tive
au•thor′i•ty
au′thor•i•za′tion
au′thor•ize′, -ized′,
  -iz′ing
au′thor•ship′
au′tism′
au•tis′tic
au′to *pl.* -tos
au′to•bahn′
au′to•bi•og′ra•pher
au′to•bi•o•graph′-
  i•cal *also* au′to•bi′-
  o•graph′ic
au′to•bi•og′ra•phy
au′to•clave′
au•toc′ra•cy
au′to•crat′
au′to•crat′ic
au′to-de•struct′
au′to•graft′
au′to•graph′

au′to•harp′
au′to•mat′
au′to•mate′, -mat′ed,
  -mat′ing
au′to•mat′ic
au′to•ma′tion
au•tom′a•tive
au•tom′a•ton
au′to•mo•bile′
au′to•mo•bil′ist
au′to•mo′tive
au′to•nom′ic
au•ton′o•mous
au•ton′o•my
au′top′sy
au′to•sug•ges′tion
au′to•troph′
au′tumn
au•tum′nal
aux•il′ia•ry
aux′in
a•vail′
a•vail′a•bil′i•ty
a•vail′a•ble
av′a•lanche′
a′vant-garde′
av′a•rice
av′a•ri′cious
a•vast′
av′a•tar′
a•venge′, a•venged′,
  a′veng•ing
av′e•nue′
a•ver′, a•verred′,
  a•ver′ring
av′er•age, -aged, -ag-
  ing

a•verse′ *(reluctant)*
  ♦*adverse*
a•ver′sion
a•vert′
a′vi•an
a′vi•a•rist
a′vi•ar′y
a′vi•ate′, -at′ed, -at′-
  ing
a′vi•a′tion
a′vi•a′tor
a′vi•a′trix
av′id
a•vid′i•ty
a′vi•on′ics
av′o•ca′do *pl.* -dos
av′o•ca′tion
av′o•cet′
a•void′
a•void′a•ble
a•void′ance
av′oir•du•pois′
a•vouch′
a•vow′
a•vow′al
a•vowed′
a•vow′ed•ly
a•vun′cu•lar
aw *interj.*
  ♦*awe*
a•wait′
a•wake′, a•woke′,
  a•waked′, a•wak′ing
a•wak′en
a•wak′en•ing
a•ward′
a•ward•ee′

a•ware'
a•wash'
a•way' *(absent)*
    ♦*aweigh*
awe *(to fill with won-
    der)*, awed, aw'ing
    ♦*aw*
a•weigh' *(clear of the
    bottom)*
    ♦*away*
awe'some
awe'-struck' *or*
    awe'-struck'en *also*
    awe'-strick'en
aw'ful
aw'ful•ly
a•while'
a•whirl'
awk'ward
awl *(tool)*
    ♦*all*
awn'ing
a•wry'
ax *or* axe, axed, ax'ing
ax'i•al
ax'i•om
ax'i•o•mat'ic *also*
    ax'i•o•mat'i•cal
ax'is *pl.* ax'es
ax'le
ax'le•tree'
ax'o•lotl'
ax'on' *also* ax'one'
aye *(affirmative)*, *also*
    ay
    ♦*eye, I*
a•zal'ea

az'i•muth
Az'tec' *also* Az'tec'an
az'ure
az'u•rite'
a•zy'gous

B

baa, baaed, baa'ing
bab'ble, -bled, -bling
bab'bler
babe
ba'bel
ba•boon'
ba•bush'ka
ba'by, -bied, -by•ing
Bab'y•lo'ni•an
ba'by's-breath' *or*
    ba'bies'-breath'
ba'by-sit', -sat', -sit'-
    ting
bac'ca•lau're•ate
bac'ca•rat'
bac'cha•nal'
bac'cha•na'lian
bach'e•lor
bach'e•lor's-but'ton
bac'il•lar'y *also* ba-
    cil'lar
ba•cil'lus *pl.* -li'
back'ache'
back'beat'
back'bite', -bit', -bit'-
    ten, -bit'ing
back'bit'er
back'board'
back'bone'

back'break'ing
back'chan'nel
back'drop'
back'er
back'field'
back'fire', -fired', -fir'-
    ing
back'-for•ma'tion
back'gam'mon
back'ground'
back'hand'
back'hand'ed
back'ing
back'lash'
back'list'
back'log'
back'pack'
back'rest'
back'side'
back'slap'per
back'slide', -slid',
    -slid' *or* -slid'den,
    -slid'ing
back'space', -spaced',
    -spac'ing
back'spin'
back'stab', -stabbed',
    -stab'bing
back'stage'
back'stairs'
back'stitch'
back'stop'
back'stretch'
back'stroke'
back'track'
back'-up' *n. & adj.*
back'ward *also* back'-

wards
back′wash′
back′wa′ter
back′woods′
ba′con
bac•te′ri•a *sing.* -ri•um
bac•te′ri•al
bac•te′ri•cid′al
bac•te′ri•cide′
bac•te′ri•o•log′ic
  also bac•te′ri•o•log′-
  i•cal
bac•te′ri•ol′o•gist
bac•te′ri•ol′o•gy
bad *(not good),* worse,
  worst
  ♦*bade*
badge
badg′er
bad′i•nage′
bad′lands′
bad′min′ton
bad′mouth′ *also* bad′-
  mouth′
baf′fle, -fled, -fling
bag, bagged, bag′ging
bag′a•telle′
ba′gel
bag′gage
bag′gy
bag′pipe′
bag′pip′er
ba•guette′
Ba•ha′mi•an
bail *(money)*
  ♦*bale*

bail *(to empty)*
  ♦*bale*
bail′iff
bail′i•wick′
bail′out′
bairn
bait *(lure)*
  ♦*bate*
baize
bake, baked, bak′ing
Ba′ke•lite′®
bak′er′s dozen
bak′er•y
ba′kla•va′
bal′a•lai′ka
bal′ance, -anced,
  -anc•ing
bal′brig′gan
bal′co•ny
bal′da•chin *also* bal′-
  da•chi′no *pl.* -nos.
bal′der•dash′
bald′-faced′
bald′head′ed
bald′ing
bald′pate′
bal′dric
bale *(to bundle),*
  baled, bal′ing
  ♦*bail*
ba•leen′
bale′ful
bal′er
Ba′li•nese′
Bal′kan
balk′y
ball *(round object,*

  dance)
  ♦*bawl*
bal′lad
bal′lad•eer′
bal′lad•ry
bal′last
bal′le•ri′na
bal′let′
bal′let′o•mane′
bal′let′o•ma′ni•a
bal•lis′tic
bal′lis•ti′cian
bal•lis′tics
bal•loon′
bal•loon′ist
bal′lot
ball′park′
ball′play′er
ball′-point′ pen
ball′room′
bal′ly•hoo′ *pl.* -hoos′
bal′ly•hoo′, -hooed′,
  -hoo′ing
balm′y
ba•lo′ney *(nonsense)*
  pl. -neys, *also* bo•lo′-
  ney
  ♦*bologna*
bal′sa
bal′sam
Bal′tic
Bal′ti•mo′re•an
bal′us•ter
bal′us•trade′
bam•bi′no *pl.* -nos *or*
  -ni
bam•boo′ *pl.* -boos′

bam·boo′zle, -zled,
 -zling
ban, banned, ban′ning
ba·nal′
ba·nal′i·ty
ba·nan′a
band *(strip, group)*
 ♦*banned*
band′age, -aged, -ag-
 ing
Band′-Aid′®
ban·dan′na *or* ban-
 dan′a
band′box′
ban·deau′ *pl.* -deaux′
 or -deaus′
ban′de·role′ *or* ban′-
 de·rol′
ban′di·coot′
ban′dit
ban′dit·ry
band′mas′ter
ban′do·leer′ *or* ban′-
 do·lier′
band′stand′
band′wag′on
ban′dy, -died, -dy·ing
ban′dy-leg′ged
bane′ful
ban′gle
bang′-up′ *adj.*
ban′ish
ban′ish·ment
ban′is·ter *also* ban′-
 nis·ter
ban′jo *pl.* -jos *or* -joes
ban′jo·ist

bank′book′
bank′er
bank′ing
bank′roll′
bank′rupt′
bank′rupt·cy
ban′ner
banns
ban′quet *(feast)*
ban·quette′ *(bench)*
ban′shee
ban′tam
ban′tam·weight′
ban′ter
ban′yan
ba′o·bab′
bap′tism
bap·tis′mal
Bap′tist
bap′tis·ter·y *also*
 bap′tis·try
bap·tize′, -tized′, -tiz′-
 ing
bar, barred, bar′ring
barb
bar·bar′i·an
bar·bar′ic
bar′ba·rism
bar·bar′i·ty
bar′ba·rous
bar′be·cue′, -cued′,
 -cu′ing
barbed
bar′bel *(feeder)*
bar′bell′ *(weight)*
bar′ber
bar′ber·ry

bar′ber·shop′
bar′bi·can
bar′bi·tal′
bar·bi′tu·rate
bar·bi′tu′ric acid
bar′ca·role′ *also* bar′-
 ca·rolle′
bard *(poet)*
 ♦*barred*
bare *(naked)*, bar′er,
 bar′est
 ♦*bear*
bare *(to uncover)*,
 bared, bar′ing
 ♦*bear*
bare′back′ *also* bare′-
 backed′
bare′faced′
bare′foot′ *also* bare′-
 foot′ed
bare′hand′ed
bare′head′ed
bare′leg′ged
bare′ly
bar′gain
barge, barged, barg′-
 ing
bar·gel′lo *pl.* -los
bar′ite′
bar′i·tone′
bar′i·um
bark *(sound, outer
 covering, ship)*
 ♦*barque*
bar′keep′er
bar′ken·tine′ *also*
 bar′quen·tine′

bark'er
bar'ley
bar'ley•corn'
bar'maid'
bar'man
bar mitz'vah
bar'na•cle
barn'storm'
barn'yard'
bar'o•graph'
ba•rom'e•ter
bar'o•met'ric *also*
  bar'o•met'ri•cal
ba•rom'e•try
bar'on *(nobleman)*
  ♦*barren*
bar'on•ess
bar'on•et
ba•ro'ni•al
bar'o•ny
ba•roque'
ba•rouche'
barque *(ship)*
  ♦*bark*
bar'racks
bar'ra•cu'da *pl.* -da
  or -das
bar'rage *(dam)*
bar•rage' *(to direct
  fire at),* -raged', -rag'-
  ing
bar'ra•try
bar'rel, -reled *or*
  -relled, -rel•ing *or*
  -rel•ling
bar'rel•house'
bar'ren *(sterile)*

♦*baron*
bar•rette'
bar'ri•cade', -cad'ed,
  -cad'ing
bar'ri•er
bar'ri•o *pl.* -os
bar'ris•ter
bar'room'
bar'row
bar'stool'
bar'tend'er
bar'ter
bar'y•on'
Bart'lett pear
bar'y•on'
bas'al
ba•salt'
ba•sal'tic
base *(bad),* bas'er, bas'-
  est
  ♦*bass (voice)*
base *(to support),*
  based, bas'ing
  ♦*bass (voice)*
base'ball'
base'board'
base'born'
base'man
base'ment
ba•sen'ji *pl.* -jis
bash
bash'ful
ba'sic *(fundamental)*
BA'SIC *(computer
  language)*
ba'si•cal•ly
bas'il

bas'i•lar *also* bas'-
  i•lar'y
ba•sil'i•ca
bas'i•lisk'
ba'sin
ba'sis *pl.* -ses'
bask *(to take pleasure)*
  ♦*basque, Basque*
bas'ket
bas'ket•ball'
bas'ket•ry
basque *(bodice)*
  ♦*bask*
Basque *(people)*
  ♦*bask*
bas'-re•lief'
bass *(fish), pl.* bass *or*
  bass'es
bass *(voice)*
  ♦*base*
bas'set
bas'si•net'
bas'so *pl.* -sos *or* -si
bas•soon'
bas•soon'ist
basso pro•fun'do *pl.*
  basso pro•fun'dos *or*
  bassi pro•fun'di
bass'wood'
bast
bas'tard•ize', -ized',
  -iz'ing
baste, bast'ed, bast'-
  ing
bas•tille' *also* bas-
  tile'
bas'ti•na'do *pl.*

-does, *also* bas'ti-
nade'
bas'tion
bat, bat'ted, bat'ting
batch
bate *(to lessen)*, bat'-
ed, bat'ing
♦*bait*
ba•teau' *pl.* -teaux'
bath *n.*
bathe, bathed, bath'-
ing
bath'er
ba•thet'ic
bath'house'
bath'mat'
bath'o•lith'
ba'thos'
bath'robe'
bath'room'
bath'tub'
bath'wa'ter
bath'y•scaph' *also*
bath'y•scaphe'
bath'y•sphere'
ba•tik'
ba•tiste'
ba•ton'
bats'man
bat•tal'ion
bat'ten
bat'ter
bat'ter•ing-ram'
bat'ter•y
bat'ting
bat'tle, -tled, -tling
bat'tle-ax' *or* bat'tle-

axe'
bat'tle•dore'
bat'tle•field'
bat'tle•front'
bat'tle•ground'
bat'tle•ment
bat'tle•ship'
bat'ty
bau'ble
baud *(unit of speed)*
♦*bawd*
baux'ite'
bawd *(prostitute)*
♦*baud*
bawd'y
bawl *(to cry)*
♦*ball*
bay *(water, recess, red-*
dish-brown color,
barking, laurel tree)
♦*bey*
bay'ber'ry
bay'o•net, -net•ed *or*
-net•ted, -net•ing *or*
-net•ting
bay'ou *pl.* -ous
bay'side'
ba•zaar' *(market)*,
also ba•zar'
♦*bizarre*
ba•zoo'ka
be *(to exist)*, present
tense am, are, is; *pl.*
are; *present*
participle be'ing;
present subjunctive
be; *past tense* was,

were; *pl.* were; *past*
participle been; *past*
subjunctive were
♦*bee*
beach *(shore)*
♦*beech*
beach'comb'er
beach'head'
bea'con
bead'ing
bea'dle
bead'work'
bead'y
bea'gle
beak
beak'er
beam
bean'bag'
bean'er•y
bean'ie
bean'pole'
bean'stalk'
bear *(animal)*
♦*bare*
bear *(to support)*,
bore, borne *or* born,
bear'ing
♦*bare*
bear'a•ble
beard'ed
bear'er
bear'ing *(mien)*
♦*baring*
bear'ish
bé'ar•naise' sauce
bear'skin'
beast'ly

beat *(to hit)*, beat,
  beat'en *or* beat,
  beat'ing
  ♦*beet*
be·a·tif'ic
be·at'i·fi·ca'tion
be·at'i·fy', -fied', -fy'-
  ing
be·at'i·tude'
beat'nik
beau *(suitor)*, *pl.* beaus
  or beaux
  ♦*bow (weapon)*
beaut
beau'tc·ous
beau·ti'cian
beau·ti·fi·ca'tion
beau'ti·ful
beau'ti·fy', -fied', -fy'-
  ing
beau'ty
beaux-arts'
bea'ver
be·calm'
be·cause'
beck'on
be·cloud'
be·come', -came',
  -come', -com'ing
bed, bed'ded, bed'-
  ding
be·daub'
be·daz'zle, -zled,
  -zling
bed'bug'
bed'cham'ber
bed'clothes'

bed'ding
be·deck'
be·dev'il
be·dew'
bed'fel'low
be·di'zen
bed'lam
bed'pan'
bed'post'
be·drag'gle, -glad,
  -gling
bed'rid'den
bed'rock'
bed'roll'
bed'room'
bed'side'
bed'sore'
bed'spread'
bed'spring'
bed'stead'
bed'time'
bee *(insect, gathering)*
  ♦*be*
beech *(tree)*
  ♦*beach*
beech'nut'
beef *pl.* beeves *or*
  beefs
beef'steak'
beef'y
bee'hive'
bee'keep'er
bee'line'
beer *(beverage)*
  ♦*bier*
bees'wax'
beet *(plant)*

♦*beat*
bee'tle *(insect, mallet)*
  ♦*betel*
be·fall', -fell', -fall'en,
  -fall'ing
be·fit', -fit'ted, -fit'-
  ting
be·fog', -fogged', -fog'-
  ging
be·fore'
be·fore'hand'
be·foul'
be·friend'
be·fud'dle, -dled,
  -dling
beg, begged, beg'ging
be·get', -got', -got'ten
  or -got', -get'ting
be·get'ter
beg'gar
be·gin', -gan', -gun',
  -gin'ning
be·gin'ner
be·go'nia
be·grime', -grimed',
  -grim'ing
be·grudge',
  -grudged', -grudg'ing
be·guile', -guiled',
  -guil'ing
be·guil'er
be·guine'
be·half'
be·have', -haved',
  -hav'ing
be·hav'ior
be·hav'ior·al

be•hav′ior•ism
be•hav′ior•ist
be•head′
be•he′moth
be•hest′
be•hind′
be•hind′hand′
be•hold′, -held′,
　-hold′ing
be•hold′en
be•hoove′, -hooved′,
　-hoov′ing
beige
be′ing
be•jew′el
be•la′bor
be•lat′ed
be•lay′
bel can′to
belch′er
bel′dam *also* bel′-
　dame
be•lea′guer
bel′fry
Bel′gian
be•lie′, -lied′, -ly′ing
be•lief′
be•li′er
be•liev′a•ble
be•lieve′, -lieved′,
　-liev′ing
be•liev′er
be•lit′tle, -tled, -tling
Be•liz′e•an *or* Be•liz′-
　i•an
bell *(instrument)*
　♦*belle*

bel′la•don′na
bell′-bot′tom
bell′-bot′toms
bell′boy′
belle *(woman)*
　♦*bell*
belles-let′tres
bell′flow′er
bell′hop′
bel′li•cose′
bel′li•cos′i•ty
bel•lig′er•ence
bel•lig′er•en•cy
bel•lig′er•ent
bel′low
bel′lows
bell′weth′er
bel′ly, -lied, -ly′ing
bel′ly•ache′, -ached′,
　-ach′ing
bel′ly•but′ton
be•long′
be•lov′ed
be•low′
belt′ing
belt′way′
be•lu′ga
bel′ve•dere′
be′ma *pl.* -ma•ta
be•mire′, -mired′,
　-mir′ing
be•moan′
be•muse′, -mused′,
　-mus′ing
bench
bench′warm′er
bend, bent, bend′ing

be•neath′
ben′e•dic′tion
ben′e•fac′tion
ben′e•fac′tor
ben′e•fice
be•nef′i•cence
be•nef′i•cent
ben′e•fi′cial
ben′e•fi′ci•ar•y
ben′e•fit
be•nev′o•lence
be•nev′o•lent
be•night′ed
be•nign′
be•nig′nant
be•nig′ni•ty
Be•nin•ese′ *pl.* -ese′
ben′i•son
ben′ny
bent
ben′thic
ben′thos′
be•numb′
Ben′ze•drine′®
ben′zene′
ben′zine′ *also* ben′zin
ben′zo•ate′
ben•zo′ic acid
ben′zol′
be•queath′
be•quest′
be•rate′, -rat′ed, -rat′-
　ing
ber•ceuse′
be•reave′, -reaved′ *or*
　-reft′, -reav′ing
be•reave′ment

be•ret'
ber'ga•mot'
ber'i•ber'i
ber•ke'li•um
Ber•mu'da shorts
Ber•noul'li's effect
ber'ry *(fruit)*
  ♦*bury*
ber•serk'
berth *(bed)*
  ♦*birth*
ber'tha
ber'yl
be•ryl'li•um
be•seech', -sought' *or*
  -seeched', -seech'ing
be•seem'
be•set', -set', -set'ting
be•side' *(next to)*
be•sides' *(in addi-
tion)*
be•siege', -sieged',
  -sieg'ing
be•smear'
be•smirch'
be•sot', -sot'ted, -sot'-
ting
be•span'gle, -gled,
  -gling
be•spat'ter
be•speak', -spoke',
  -spok'en *or* -spoke',
  -speak'ing
be•spec'ta•cled
be•spread', -spread',
  -spread'ing
be•sprin'kle, -kled,

-kling
best
bes'tial
bes•ti•al'i•ty
bes'ti•ar'y
be•stir', -stirred',
  -stir'ring
be•stow'
be•strew', -strewed',
  -strewed' *or*
  -strewn', -strew'ing
be•stride', -strode',
  -strid'den, -strid'ing
best'-sell'ing
bet, bet, bet'ting
be'ta
be•take', -took', -tak'-
  en, -tak'ing
be'ta•tron'
be'tel *(plant)*
  ♦*beetle*
bête noire'
be•think', -thought',
  -think'ing
be•tide', -tid'ed, -tid'-
ing
be•times'
be•to'ken
be•tray'
be•troth'
be•troth'al
be•trothed'
bet'ter *(greater)*
  ♦*bettor*
bet'ter•ment
bet'tor *(one who bets)*
  ♦*better*

be•tween'
be•twixt'
bev'a•tron'
bev'el, -eled *or* -elled,
  -el'ing *or* -el'ling
bev'er•age
bev'y
be•wail'
be•ware', -wared',
  -war'ing
be•wil'der
be•witch'
bey *(governor)*
  ♦*bay*
be•yond'
bez'el
be•zique'
Bhu•tan•ese' *pl.* -ese'
bi•a'ly *pl.* -lys
bi•an'nu•al *(twice a
year)*
  ♦*biennial,
semiannual*
bi'as, -ased *or* -assed,
  -as•ing *or* -as•sing
bi•ath'lon
bi•ax'i•al
bib, bibbed, bib'bing
bi'be•lot
Bi'ble
Bib'li•cal *also* bib'li-
cal
bib'li•og'ra•pher
bib'li•o•graph'i•cal
  also bib'li•o•graph'-
ic
bib'li•og'ra•phy

bib'li•o•ma'ni•a

bib'li•o•ma'ni•ac'

bib'li•o•phile'

bib'u•lous

bi•cam'er•al

bi•car'bon•ate'

bi'cen•ten'a•ry

bi'cen•ten'ni•al

bi'ceps' *pl.* -ceps' *or* -ceps'es

bi•chlo'ride

bick'er

bi•coast'al

bi'col•or *also* bi'col'-ored

bi'con•cave'

bi•con•vex'

bi•cus'pid

bi'cy•cle, -cled, -cling

bi'cy•clist

bid *(to order, invite),* bade, bid'den *or* bid, bid'ding

bid *(to strive, offer),* bid, bid'ding

bid'der

bid'ding

bid'dy

bide, bid'ed *or* bode, bid'ed, bid'ing

bi•den'tate'

bi•det'

bi•en'ni•al *(once in two years)*

♦*biannual, semiannual*

bier *(coffin stand)*

♦*beer*

bi•fo'cal

bi'fur•cate', -cat'ed, -cat'ing

bi'fur•ca'tion

big, big'ger, big'gest

big'a•mist

big'a•mous

big'a•my

Big Dip'per

big'-heart'ed

big'horn'

bight *(loop, bay)*

♦*bite, byte*

big'ot

big'ot•ed

big'ot•ry

big'wig'

bi'jou' *pl.* -joux'

bike, biked, bik'ing

bike'way'

bi•ki'ni

bi•lat'er•al

bile

bilge, bilged, bilg'ing

bi•lin'gual

bil'ious

bilk'er

bill'board'

bil'let

bil'let-doux' *pl.* bil'-lets-doux'

bill'fold'

bill'hook'

bil'liard

bil'liards

bill'ing

bil'lings•gate'

bil'lion

bil'lion•aire'

bil'lionth

bil'low

bil'ly

bi•me•tal'lic

bi•met'al•lism

bi•met'al•list

bi•month'ly *(once in two months)*

♦*semimonthly*

bin *(container)*

♦*been*

bi'na•ry

bin•au'ral

bind, bound, bind'ing

bind'er

bind'er•y

bind'weed'

binge

bin'go

bin'na•cle

bin•oc'u•lar

bi•no'mi•al

bi'o-as'say'

bi'o•as'tro•nau'tics

bi'o•chem'i•cal *also* bi'o•chem'ic

bi'o•chem'ist

bi'o•chem'is•try

bi'o•de•grad'a•ble

bi'o•en'gi•neer'ing

bi'o•feed'back'

bi'o•gen'e•sis

bi'o•ge'o•graph'ic *also* bi'o•ge'o•graph'-

i•cal
bi'o•ge•og'ra•phy
bi•og'ra•pher
bi'o•graph'i•cal *also*
　bi'o•graph'ic
bi•og'ra•phy
bi'o•log'i•cal *also* bi'-
　o•log'ic
bi•ol'o•gist
bi•ol'o•gy
bi'o•lu'mi•nes'-
　cence
bi'o•lu'mi•nes'cent
bi'ome'
bi'o•med'i•cine
bi'o•met'rics
bi•on'ics
bi'o•phys'i•cist
bi'o•phys'ics
bi•op'ic
bi•op'sic
bi'op'sy
bi'o•rhythm'
bi'o•rhyth'mic
bi•os'co•py *pl.* -pies
bi'o•sphere'
bi'o•syn'the•sis
bi'o•syn•thet'ic
bi•o'ta
bi•ot'ic
bi'o•tin
bi•par'ti•san
bi•par'ti•san•ism
bi•par'tite'
bi•par•ti'tion
bi'ped'
bi'plane'

bi•po'lar
bi•ra'cial
bi•ra'cial•ism
birch
bird'bath'
bird'brain'
bird'cage'
bird'call'
bird'house'
bird'ie
bird'lime'
bird'seed'
bird's'-eye'
bi•ret'ta
birr *(whirring sound)*
　♦*bur, burr*
birth *(beginning)*
　♦*berth*
birth'day'
birth'mark'
birth'place'
birth'rate'
birth'right'
birth'stone'
bis'cuit
bi'sect'
bi•sec'tion
bi•sec'tor
bi•sex'u•al
bish'op
bish'op•ric
bis'muth
bi'son
bisque
bis'tro *pl.* -tros
bi•sul'fate'
bit

bite *(to cut or tear)*,
　bit, bit'ten *or* bit,
　bit'ing
　♦*bight, byte*
bit'ter
bit'tern
bit'ter•root'
bit'ters
bit'ter•sweet'
bi•tu'men
bi•tu'mi•nous
bi•va'lent
bi'valve'
biv'ou•ac, -acked,
　-ack•ing
bi•week'ly *(once in
　two weeks)*
　♦*semiweekly*
bi•year'ly *(once in
　two years)*
　♦*semiyearly*
bi•zarre' *(odd)*
　♦*bazaar*
blab, blabbed, blab'-
　bing
blab'ber
blab'ber•mouth'
blab'by
black'-and-blue' *adj.*
black'ball'
black'ber'ry
black'bird'
black'board'
black'bod'y
black'cap'
black'damp'
black'en

black'-eyed' pea
black'-eyed' Su'san
black'guard
black'head'
black'ing
black'jack'
black'list'
black'mail'
black'-mar'ket v.
black'out' n.
black'smith'
black'snake'
black'thorn'
black'top', -topped',
  -top'ping
blad'der
blade
blad'ed
blah
blain
blam'a•ble also
  blame'a•ble
blame, blamed, blam'-
  ing
blame'less
blam'er
blame'wor'thy
blanch (to whiten),
  also blench
blanc•mange'
bland
blan'dish
bland'ly
blan'ket
blank'ly
blare, blared, blar'ing
blar'ney

bla•sé'
blas•pheme',
  -phemed', -phem'ing
blas'phe•mous
blas'phe•my
blast'off' n., also
  blast'-off'
blas'tu•la pl. -las or
  -lae'
bla'tan•cy
bla'tant
blath'er
blath'er•skite'
blaze, blazed, blaz'ing
blaz'er
bla'zon
bleach
bleach'ers
bleak'ly
blear'y
blear'y-eyed'
bleat'er
bleed, bled, bleed'ing
bleed'er
bleed'ing-heart'
bleep
blem'ish
blench (to shy away)
  ♦blanch
blend'er
bless, blessed or blest,
  bless'ing
bless'ed adj.
blight
blimp
blind'ers
blind'fold'

blink'er
blintz also blin'tze
blip'
bliss'ful
blis'ter
blithe, blith'er, blith'-
  est
blitz
blitz'krieg'
bliz'zard
bloat
blob
bloc (group)
block (solid substance)
block•ade', -ad'ed,
  -ad'ing
block•ade'-run'ner
block'age
block'bust'er
block'head'
block'house'
bloke
blond fem. blonde
blood'cur'dling
blood'ed
blood'hound'
blood'less
blood'let'ting
blood'line'
blood'mo•bile'
blood'root'
blood'shed'
blood'shot'
blood'stain'
blood'stone'
blood stream also
  blood'stream'

blood'suck'er
blood'thirst'y
blood'y, -ied, -y•ing
bloom'er
bloop'er
blos'som
blot, blot'ted, blot'ting
blotch
blot'ter
blouse, bloused,
    blous'ing
blow, blew, blown,
    blow'ing
blow'-dry', -dried',
    -dry'ing
blow'er
blow'fish' *pl.* -fish' *or*
    -fish'es
blow'gun'
blow'hard'
blow'hole'
blow'off '
blow'out' *n.*
blow'pipe'
blow'torch'
blow'up' *n.*
blow'zy *also* blow'sy
blub'ber
bludg'eon
blue *(of the color
    blue),* blu'er, blu'est
    ♦*blew*
blue *(to color),* blued,
    blu'ing
    ♦*blew*
blue'bell'
blue'ber'ry

blue'bird'
blue'bon'net
blue book *also* blue'-
    book'
blue'bot'tle
blue'-chip' *adj.*
blue'-col'lar *adj.*
blue'fish' *pl.* -fish' *or*
    -fish'es
blue'grass'
blue'jack'et
blue'nose'
blue'-pen'cil, -ciled
    or -cilled, -cil•ing *or*
    -cil•ling
blue'print'
blue'-rib'bon *adj.*
blues
blue'stock'ing
blu'ets
bluff 'er
blu'ing *also* blue'ing
blu'ish *also* blue'ish
blun'der
blun'der•buss'
blunt'ly
blur, blurred, blur'ring
blurb
blur'ry
blurt
blush'er
blus'ter
blus'ter•y *also* blus'-
    ter•ous
bo'a
boar *(animal)*
    ♦*bore*

board *(piece of wood)*
    ♦*bored*
board'er *(lodger)*
    ♦*border*
board'ing house *also*
    board'ing•house'
board'room'
board'walk'
boast'ful
boat'house'
boat'load'
boat'man
boat'swain *also* bo''-
    s'n, bo'sun
bob, bobbed, bob'bing
bob'bin
bob'ble, -bled, -bling
bob'by
bob'by•sox'er
bob'cat'
bob'o•link'
bob'sled', -sled'ded,
    -sled'ding
bob'tail'
bob•white'
bode, bod'ed, bod'ing
bod'ice
bod'i•ly
bod'kin
bod'y
bod'y•build'er
bod'y•guard'
bod'y•surf '
bog, bogged, bog'ging
bo'gey *(golf score),* pl.
    -geys
    ♦*bogie, bogy*

bog'gle, -gled, -gling
bog'gy
bo'gie *(railroad car)*,
  also bo'gy
  ♦*bogey*
bo'gus
bo'gy *(hobgoblin), also*
  bo'gey, bo'gie
Bo•he'mi•an *also*
  bo•he'mi•an
boil'er
boil'er•mak'er
bois'ter•ous
bo'la *also* bo'las
bold'face', -faced',
  -fac'ing
bold'-faced' *adj.*
bold'ly
bole *(tree trunk)*
  ♦*boll, bowl*
bo•le'ro *pl.* -ros
Bo•liv'i•an
boll *(seed pod)*
  ♦*bole, bowl*
bol'lix
bo•lo'gna *(meat),*
  also ba•lo'ney, bo-
  lo'ney
Bol'she•vik'
Bol'she•vism
bol'ster
bolt'er
bo'lus *pl.* -lus•es
bomb
bom•bard'
bom'bar•dier'
bom•bard'ment

bom'bast'
bom•bas'tic
bom'ba•zine'
bomb'er
bomb'proof'
bomb'shell'
bomb'sight'
bo'na fide'
bo•nan'za
bon'bon'
bond'age
bond'hold'er
bond'ing
bond'ser'vant
bonds'man
bone, boned, bon'ing
bone'black'
bone'-dry'
bone'fish' *pl.* -fish' or
  -fish'es
bone'head'
bon'er
bon'fire'
bong
bon'go *pl.* -gos
bon'ho•mie'
bo•ni'to *pl.* -to *or* -tos
bon' mot' *pl.* bons'
  mots'
bon'net
bon'ny *also* bon'nie
bon•sai' *pl.* -sai'
bo'nus *pl.* -nus•es
bon vi•vant' *pl.* bons
  vi•vants'
bon voy•age'
bon'y

boo *pl.* boos
boo, booed, boo'ing
boo'-boo *pl.* -boos
boo'by
boo'dle, -dled, -dling
boog'ie-woog'ie
book'bind'er•y
book'bind'ing
book'case'
book'end' *also* book
  end
book'ie
book'ing
book'ish
book'keep'er
book'keep'ing
book'let
book'mak'er
book'mark'
book'mo•bile'
book'plate'
book'rack'
book'sell'er
book'shelf'
book'stall'
book'stand'
book'store'
book'worm'
boom
boo'mer•ang'
boom'town'
boon'docks'
boon'dog'gle, -gled,
  -gling
boor'ish
boost'er
boot'black'

boot'ee *(baby shoe),*
   also boot'ie
   ♦*booty*
booth *pl.* booths
boot'jack'
boot'leg', -legged',
   -leg'ging
boot'leg'ger
boot'lick'
boot'strap'
boo'ty *(plunder)*
   ♦*bootee*
booze, boozed, booz'-
   ing
booz'er
booz'y
bop, bopped, bop'ping
bo'rate'
bo'rax'
Bor•deaux' *pl.*
   -deaux
bor•del'lo *pl.* -los
bor'der *(margin)*
   ♦*boarder*
bor'der•land'
bor'der•line'
bore *(to drill, tire),*
   bored, bor'ing
   ♦*boar*
bore *(wave)*
   ♦*boar*
bo're•al
bore'dom
bore'hole'
bor'er
bo'ric
bor'ing

born *(brought into
   life)*
   ♦*borne, bourn*
born'-a•gain' *adj.*
borne *(carried)*
   ♦*born, bourn*
bo'ron'
bor'ough *(town)*
   ♦*burro, burrow*
bor'row
borscht *also* borsht,
   borsch
bor'zoi'
bosh
bosk'y
bos'om
bo'son
boss'ism
boss'y
bo•tan'i•cal *also* bo-
   tan'ic
bot'a•nist
bot'a•ny
botch'er
bot'fly'
both
both'er
both'er•a'tion
both'er•some
bot'tle, -tled, -tling
bot'tle•neck'
bot'tle-nosed'
   dolphin
bot'tom
bot'tom•less
bot'tom•most'
bot'u•lism'

bou'doir'
bouf•fant'
bou'gain•vil'le•a
bough *(branch)*
   ♦*bow (section of a
   ship, a bending)*
bouil'la•baisse'
bouil'lon' *(broth)*
   ♦*bullion*
boul'der *(rock)*
   ♦*bolder*
boul'e•vard'
bounce, bounced,
   bounc'ing
bounc'er
bound
bound'a•ry
bound'en
bound'er
boun'te•ous
boun'ti•ful
boun'ty
bou•quet'
bour'bon
bour•geois' *pl.* -geois'
bour•geoi'sie'
bour•geois'i•fi•ca'-
   tion
bour•geois'i•fy',
   -fied', -fy'ing
bourn *(stream), also*
   bourne
   ♦*born, borne*
bourse
bout
bou•tique'
bou'ton•niere' *also*

bou•ton•nière'
bo'vine'
bow (section of a ship,
   a bending)
  ◆bough
bow (weapon)
  ◆beau
bowd'ler•i•za'tion
bowd'ler•ize', -ized',
  -iz'ing
bow'el
bow'er
bow'fin'
bow'ie knife
bowl (dish, ball,
  game)
  ◆bole, boll
bow'leg'
bow'leg'ged
bow'ler
bow'line
bowl'ing
bow'sprit'
bow'string'
bow'-wow'
box'car'
box'er
box'ing
box'-of'fice adj.
box'wood'
boy (male child)
  ◆buoy
boy'cott'
boy'friend'
boy'hood'
boy'sen•ber'ry
bra

brace, braced, brac'-
  ing
brace'let
brac'er
brach'i•o•pod'
brack'en
brack'et
brack'ish
bract
brad
brae (hillside)
  ◆bray
brag, bragged, brag'-
  ging
brag'ga•do'ci•o pl.
  -os
brag'gart
brag'ger
Brah'ma
Brah'man also Brah'-
  min
braid'ing
Braille also braille
brain'pan'
brain'storm'
brain'teas'er
brain'wash'
brain'work'
brain'y
braise (to cook),
  braised, brais'ing
  ◆braze
brake (fern, thicket)
  ◆break
brake (to reduce),
  braked, brak'ing
  ◆break

brake'age
bram'ble
bram'bly
bran
branch
branch'let
bran'dish
brand'-new'
bran'dy, -died, -dy-
  ing
brant pl. brant or
  brants
brash'ly
bras•siere' or bras-
  sière'
brass'ware'
brass'y
brat'ty
brat'wurst'
bra•va'do pl. -does or
  -dos
brave, brav'er, brav'-
  est
brave, braved, brav'-
  ing
brav'er•y
bra'vo pl. -voes or
  -vos
bra•vu'ra
brawl'er
brawn'y
bray (harsh cry)
  ◆brae
bray'er
braze (to solder),
  brazed, braz'ing
  ◆braise

bra'zen
bra'zier
Bra•zil'ian
Bra•zil' nut
breach *(violation, gap)*
  ♦*breech*
bread *(food)*
  ♦*bred*
bread'-and-but'ter
  adj.
bread'bas'ket
bread'board'
bread'box'
bread'fruit'
bread'stuff'
breadth *(width)*
  ♦*breath*
bread'win'ner
break *(to crack),*
  broke, bro'ken,
  break'ing
  ♦*brake*
break'a•ble
break'age
break'down' *n.*
break'er
break'fast
break'front'
break'neck' *adj.*
break'point'
break'through' *n.*
break'up' *n.*
break'wa'ter
bream *pl.* bream *or*
  breams
breast'bone'
breast'plate'

breast'work'
breath *(air)*
  ♦*breadth*
breath'a•ble
Breath'a•lyz'er®
breathe, breathed,
  breath'ing
breath'er
breath'less
breath'tak'ing
breath'y
breech *(buttocks)*
  ♦*breach*
breech'cloth'
breech'es
breech'load'er
breed, bred, breed'ing
breed'er
breeze, breezed,
  breez'ing
breeze'way'
breez'y
breth'ren
bre•vet'
bre'vi•ar•y
brev'i•ty
brew'er
brew'er•y
brew'ing
bri'ar *(shrub, pipe),*
  also bri'er
bribe, bribed, brib'ing
brib'er•y
bric'-a-brac'
brick'bat'
brick'lay'er
brick'work'

brick'yard'
bri'dal *(wedding)*
  ♦*bridle*
bride'groom'
brides'maid'
bridge, bridged, bridg'-
  ing
bridge'a•ble
bridge'head'
bridge'work'
bri'dle *(to restrain),*
  -dled, -dling
  ♦*bridal*
Brie
brief'case'
brief'ing
bri'er *(plant), also* bri'-
  ar
brig
bri•gade'
brig'a•dier' general
  pl. brig'a•dier'
  generals
brig'and
brig'and•age
brig'an•tine'
bright'en
bright'ness
bril'liance *also* bril'-
  lian•cy
bril'liant
bril'lian•tine'
brim'ful'
brim'less
brim'stone'
brin'dle
brin'dled

brine
bring, brought, bring'-
 ing
brink
brin'y
bri'o
bri•oche'
bri•quette' also bri-
 quet'
bris'ket
brisk'ly
bris'ling
bris'tle, -tled, -tling
bris'tly
bri•tan'nia metal
britch'es
Brit'i•cism also Brit'-
 ish•ism
Brit'ish
Brit'on (person)
 ♦Britain
brit'tle
broach (to introduce)
 ♦brooch
broad'ax' also broad'-
 axe'
broad'cast', -cast' or
 -cast'ed, -cast'ing
broad'cloth'
broad'en
broad'leaf'
broad'-leaved' also
 broad'-leafed'
broad'loom'
broad'-mind'ed
broad'side'
broad'sword'

broad'tail'
Broad'way'
bro•cade', -cad'ed,
 -cad'ing
broc'co•li
bro•chette'
bro•chure'
bro'gan
brogue
broil'er
bro'ken
bro'ken-down'
bro'ken•heart'ed
bro'ker
bro'ker•age
bro•me'li•ad'
bro'mic acid
bro'mide'
bro•mid'ic
bro'mine'
bron'chi•a sing. -chi-
 um
bron'chi•al
bron'chi•ole'
bron•chi'tis
bron'cho•pneu-
 mon'ia
bron'cho•scope'
bron'chus pl. -chi'
bron'co pl. -cos
bron'co•bust'er
bron'to•saur' also
 bron'to•sau'rus
bronze, bronzed,
 bronz'ing
brooch (pin)
 ♦broach

brood'er
brood'y
brook
broom (sweeper)
 ♦brougham
broom'corn'
broom'stick'
broth
broth'el
broth'er
broth'er•hood'
broth'er-in-law' pl.
 broth'ers-in-law
brougham (carriage)
 ♦broom
brou'ha•ha'
brow'beat', -beat',
 -beat'en, -beat'ing
brown'ie
brown'nose', -nosed',
 -nos'ing
brown'out' n.
brown'stone'
browse, browsed,
 brows'ing
bru'cel•lo'sis
bru'in
bruise (to injure),
 bruised, bruis'ing
 ♦brews
bruis'er
bruit (to spread news)
 ♦brute
brunch
bru•net' fem. bru-
 nette'
brunt

brush'fire'
brush'-off' *n.*
brush'wood'
brush'work'
brusque *also* brusk
Brus'sels sprouts
bru'tal
bru•tal'i•ty
bru'tal•ize', -ized',
  -iz'ing
brute *(beast)*
  ♦*bruit*
brut'ish
bry'o•phyte'
bub'ble, -bled, -bling
bub'bly
bu'bo *pl.* -boes
bu•bon'ic
buc'ca•neer'
buck'a•roo' *pl.*
  -roos', *also* buck'er-
  oo' *pl.* -oos
buck'board'
buck'et
buck'eye'
buck'le, -led, -ling
buck'ler
buck'ram
buck'saw'
buck'shot'
buck'skin'
buck'tooth' *pl.* -teeth'
buck'toothed'
buck'wheat'
bu•col'ic
bud, bud'ded, bud'-
  ding

bud'der
Bud'dha
Bud'dhism
Bud'dhist
bud'dy
budge, budged, budg'-
  ing
budg'er•i•gar'
budg'et
budg'et•ar'y
buff
buf'fa•lo' *also* -loes'
  or -los' *or* -lo
buff'er
buf•fet' *(sideboard)*
buf'fet *(blow)*
buf'fle•head'
buf•foon'
buf•foon'er•y
bug, bugged, bug'ging
bug'a•boo' *pl.* -boos'
bug'bear'
bug'-eyed'
bug'ger
bug'gy
bu'gle, -gled, -gling
bu'gler
build *(to erect)*, built,
  build'ing
  ♦*billed*
build'a•ble
build'er
build'ing
build'-up' *n.*, *also*
  build'up'
built'-in'
built'-up'

bulb
bul'bar
bul'bous
bul'bul'
Bul•gar'i•an
bulge, bulged, bulg'-
  ing
bulg'y
bu•lim'i•a
bu•lim'ic
bulk'head'
bulk'y
bull'dog', -dogged',
  -dog'ging
bull'doze', -dozed',
  -doz'ing
bull'doz'er
bul'let
bul'le•tin
bul'let•proof'
bull'fight'
bull'fight'er
bull'finch'
bull'frog'
bull'head'
bull'head'ed
bul'lion *(metal)*
  ♦*bouillon*
bull'ish
bull'necked'
bul'lock
bull'pen'
bull'ring'
bull'roar'er
bull's eye *also*
  bull's'-eye'
bull'whip',

-whipped', -whip'-
ping
bul'ly, -lied, -ly•ing
bul'ly•boy'
bul'rush'
bul'wark
bum, bummed, bum'-
ming
bum'ber•shoot'
bum'ble, -bled, -bling
bum'ble•bee'
bump'er
bump'kin
bump'tious
bump'y
bun
bunch'y
bun'co pl. -cos, also
bun'ko pl. -kos
bun'dle, -dled, -dling
bun'ga•low'
bung'hole'
bun'gle, -gled, -gling
bun'ion
bunk
bun'ker
bunk'house'
bun'kum also bun'-
combe
bun'ny
Bun'sen burner
bunt'ing
bunt'line
buoy (float)
  ♦boy
buoy•an•cy
buoy'ant

bur (prickly seed), also
burr
  ♦birr
bur'ble', -bled, -bling
bur'den
bur'den•some
bur'dock'
bu'reau pl. -reaus or
reaux
bu•reauc'ra•cy
bu'reau•crat'
bu'reau•crat'ic
bu•reauc'ra•ti•za'-
tion
bu•reauc'ra•tize',
-tized', -tiz'ing
bu•rette' also bu•ret'
burg (town)
  ♦burgh
bur'geon
burg'er (hamburger)
  ♦burgher
bur'gess
burgh (town)
  ♦burg
burgh'er (citizen)
  ♦burger
bur'glar
bur'glar•ize', -ized',
-iz'ing
bur'gla•ry
bur'gle, -gled, -gling
bur'go•mas'ter
bur'gun•dy (red col-
or)
Bur'gun•dy (wine)
bur'i•al

bu'rin
burl
bur'lap'
bur•lesque',
-lesqued', -lesqu'ing
bur'ly
Bur•mese' adj., also
Bur'man
Bur•mese' pl. -mese'
burn, burned or
burnt, burn'ing
burn'er
bur'nish
bur•noose' also bur-
nous'
burn'out' n.
burp
burr (edge, trill, wash-
er), also bur
  ♦birr, bur
bur'ro (donkey), pl.
-ros
  ♦borough, burrow
bur'row (hole)
  ♦borough, burro
bur'sa' pl. -sae or -sas
bur'sar
bur•si'tis
burst, burst, burst'ing
bur'y (to inter), -ied,
-y•ing
  ♦berry
bus (motor vehicle), pl.
bus'es or bus'ses
  ♦buss
bus (to transport),
bused or bussed,

bus'ing *or* bus'sing
 ♦*buss*
bus'by
bushed
bush'el
bush'ing
bush'-league' *adj.*
bush'mas'ter
bush'whack'
bush'y
busi'ness
busi'ness•like'
busi'ness•man'
busi'ness•wom'an
bus'kin
buss *(kiss)*
 ♦*bus*
bus'tard
bust'er
bus•tier'
bus'tle, -tled, -tling
bust'y
bus'y, -ied, -y•ing
bus'y•bod'y
but *conj.*
 ♦*butt*
bu'ta•di'ene'
bu'tane'
butch'er
butch'er•y
but'ler
butt *(target, end)*
 ♦*but*
butt *(to hit, join)*
 ♦*but*
butte
but'ter

but'ter-and-eggs'
but'ter•cup'
but'ter•fat'
but'ter•fin'gered
but'ter•fin'gers
but'ter•fish' *pl.* -fish'
 or -fish'es
but'ter•fly'
but'ter•milk'
but'ter•nut'
but'ter•scotch'
but'ter•y
but'tock
but'ton
but'ton•hole',
 -holed', -hol'ing
but'ton•hook'
but'ton•wood'
but'tress
but'tyl
bu•tyr'ic
bux'om
buy *(to purchase)*,
 bought, buy'ing
 ♦*by, bye*
buy'back' *n.*
buy'er
buy'out' *n.*
buz'zard
buzz'er
by *prep.*
 ♦*buy, bye*
by'-and-by' *n.*
bye *(position)*
 ♦*buy, by*
bye'-bye'
by'-e•lec'tion *also*

bye'-e•lec'tion
by'gone'
by'law'
by'-line', -lined', -lin'-
 ing, *also* by'line'
by'-lin'er
by'-pass' *also* by'pass'
by'-path'
by'-play'
by'-prod'uct
by'road'
bys'sus *pl.* -sus•es *or*
 -si'
by'stand'er
byte *(computer unit)*
 ♦*bight, bite*
by'way'
by'word'
Byz'an•tine'

C

cab
ca•bal', -balled', -ball'-
 ing
cab'al•le'ro *pl.* -ros
ca•ban'a *also* ca•ba'-
 ña
cab'a•ret'
cab'bage
cab'by
cab'driv'er
cab'in
cab'i•net
cab'i•net•mak'er

cab'i•net•work'
ca'ble, -bled, -bling
ca'ble•cast', -cast',
    -cast'ing
ca'ble•gram'
ca'ble•vi'sion
cab'o•chon'
ca•boo'dle
ca•boose'
ca•ca'o *pl.* -os
cach'a•lot'
cache *(to hide)*,
    cached, cach'ing
    ♦*cash*
ca•chet'
cack'le, -led, -ling
cac'o•mis'tle
ca•coph'o•nous
ca•coph'o•ny
cac'tus *pl.* -ti' *or* -tus-
    es
cad
ca•dav'er
ca•dav'er•ous
cad'die *(to carry golf
    clubs)*, -died, -dy-
    ing, *also* cad'dy
cad'dis fly *also* cad'-
    dice fly
cad'dish
cad'dy *(box)*
    ♦*caddie*
ca'dence
ca•den'za
ca•det'
cadge, cadged, cadg'-
    ing

cad'mic
cad'mi•um
cad're
ca•du'ce•us *pl.* -ce•i'
Cae•sar'e•an *also*
    cae•sar'e•an section
cae•su'ra *pl.* -ras *or*
    -rae
cae•su'ral *also* cae-
    su'ric
ca•fé'
caf'e•te'ri•a
caf•feine' *also* caf-
    fein'
caf'tan
cage, caged, cag'ing
cag'ey *also* cag'y
ca•hoots'
cai'man *pl.* -mans,
    also cay'man
cairn
cairn'gorm'
Cairn terrier
cais'son'
cai'tiff
ca•jole', -joled', -jol'-
    ing
ca•jol'er•y
cake, caked, cak'ing
cake'walk'
cal'a•bash'
cal'a•boose'
ca•la'di•um
ca'la•ma'ri *pl.* -ris
cal'a•mine'
ca•lam'i•tous
ca•lam'i•ty

cal•car'e•ous
cal•cif'er•ous
cal'ci•fi•ca'tion
cal'ci•fy', -fied', -fy'-
    ing
cal'ci•mine'
cal'ci•na'tion
cal'cine', -cined', -cin'-
    ing
cal'cite'
cal•cit'ic
cal'ci•um
cal'cu•la•ble
cal'cu•late', -lat'ed,
    -lat'ing
cal'cu•la'tion
cal'cu•la'tor
cal'cu•lus *pl.* -li' *or*
    -lus•es
cal'dron *also* caul'-
    dron
cal'en•dar *(time)*
cal'en•der *(press)*
cal'ends *pl.* -ends
calf *pl.* calves
calf'skin'
cal'i•ber
cal'i•brate', -brat'ed,
    -brat'ing
cal'i•bra'tion
cal'i•bra'tor
cal'i•co *pl.* -coes *or*
    -cos
Cal'i•for'nian
cal'i•for'ni•um
cal'i•per *also* cal'li-
    per

ca'liph *also* ca'lif
ca'liph•ate'
cal'is•then'ics
cal'la
call'board'
call'er
cal•lig'ra•pher *also*
  cal•lig'ra•phist
cal'li•graph'ic
cal•lig'ra•phy
call'ing
cal•li'o•pe'
cal•los'i•ty
cal'lous *(unfeeling)*
  ♦callus
cal'low
cal'lus *(hard tissue)*
  ♦callous
calm'ly
cal'o•mel'
ca•lor'ic
cal'o•rie
cal'o•rif'ic
cal'o•rim'e•ter
cal'u•met'
ca•lum'ni•ate', -at'-
  ed, -at'ing
ca•lum'ni•a'tion
ca•lum'ni•a'tor
ca•lum'ni•ous
cal'um•ny
cal'va•ry
calve, calved, calv'ing
Cal'vin•ism
Cal'vin•ist
ca•lyp'so
ca'lyx *pl.* -lyx•es *or*

-ly•ces'
cam
ca'ma•ra'de•rie
cam'as *also* cam'ass
cam'ber
cam'bi•um
Cam•bo'di•an
cam'bric
cam'cord'er
cam'el
ca•mel'lia
ca•mel'o•pard'
Cam'e•lot'
cam'el's-hair' *adj.*
Cam'em•bert'
cam'e•o' *pl.* -os'
cam'er•a
cam'er•al
cam'er•a•man'
cam'i•sole'
cam'ou•flage',
  -flaged', -flag'ing
cam'ou•flag'er
cam•paign'
cam•pa•ni'le *pl.* -les
  or -li
camp'fire'
camp'ground'
cam'pe•si'no *pl.* -nos
cam'phor
cam'phor•ate', -at'-
  ed, -at'ing
cam•phor'ic
camp'site'
cam'pus *pl.* -pus•es
cam'shaft'
can *auxiliary, past*

tense could
can *(to preserve)*,
  canned, can'ning
Ca•na'di•an
ca•naille'
ca•nal'
ca•nal'i•za'tion
ca•nal'ize', -ized',
  -iz'ing
can'a•pé' *(appetizer)*
  ♦canopy
ca•nard'
ca•nar'y
ca•nas'ta
can'can'
can'cel, -celed *or*
  -celled, -cel'ing *or*
  -cel'ling
can'cel•a•ble
can'cel•la'tion *also*
  can'ce•la'tion
can'cer *(tumor)*
Can'cer *(constella-
  tion)*
can'cer•ous
can•del'a
can'de•la'brum *pl.*
  -bra *or* -brums, *also*
  can'de•la'bra *pl.*
  -bras
can'did
can'di•da•cy *also*
  can'di•da•ture'
can'di•date'
can'died
can'dle
can'dle•hold'er

can'dle•light'
can'dle•pin'
can'dle•pow'er
can'dle•stick'
can'dle•wick'
can'dor
can'dy, -died, -dy•ing
cane, caned, can'ing
cane'brake'
can'er
ca'nine'
can'is•ter
can'ker
can'ker•ous
can'ker•worm'
can'na
can'na•bis
can'nel
can'nel•¹o'ni
can'ner•y
can'ni•bal
can'ni•bal•ism
can'ni•bal•is'tic
can'ni•bal•i•za'tion
can'ni•bal•ize', -ized', -iz'ing
can'ning
can'non (gun), pl. -non or -nons
♦*canon*
can'non•ade', -ad'ed, -ad'ing
can'non•ball'
can'non•eer'
can'not
can'ny
ca•noe', -noed', -noe'-

ing
ca•noe'ist
can'on (ecclesiastical law, clergyman)
♦*cannon*
ca•non'i•cal also ca-non'ic
can'on•ic'i•ty
can'on•i•za'tion
can'on•ize', -ized', -iz'ing
can'o•py (to cover), -pied, -py'ing
♦*canapé*
cant (slope, whining speech)
can't contraction
can'ta•bi•le'
can'ta•loupe' also can'ta•loup'
can•tan'ker•ous
can•ta'ta
can•teen'
can'ter (gait)
♦*cantor*
Can'ter•bur'y bells
can'thus pl. -thi'
can'ti•cle
can'ti•le'ver
can•ti'na
can'tle
can'to pl. -tos
can'ton
Can'ton•ese' pl. -ese'
can'tor (singer)
♦*canter*
Ca•nuck'

can'vas (fabric)
♦*canvass*
can'vas•back'
can'vass (poll)
♦*canvas*
can'yon
cap, capped, cap'ping
ca•pa•bil'i•ty
ca'pa•ble
ca•pa'cious
ca•pac'i•tance
ca•pac'i•tate', -tat'-ed, -tat'ing
ca•pac'i•tive
ca•pac'i•tor
ca•pac'i•ty
ca•par'i•son
ca'per
cape'skin'
cap'il•lar'i•ty
cap'il•lar'y
cap'i•tal (city, wealth, top of a column)
♦*capitol*
cap'i•tal•ism
cap'i•tal•ist
cap'i•tal•is'tic
cap'i•tal•i•za'tion
cap'i•tal•ize', -ized', -iz'ing
cap'i•ta'tion
cap'i•tol (building)
♦*capital*
ca•pit'u•late', -lat'-ed, -lat'ing
ca•pit'u•la'tion
ca•pit'u•la'tor

ca•pit'u•la•to'ry
cap'let
ca'pon'
ca•pric'cio *pl.* -cios
　or -ci
ca•price'
ca•pri'cious
Cap'ri•corn'
cap'ri•ole', -oled',
　-ol'ing
cap'size', -sized', -siz'-
　ing
cap'stan
cap'stone'
cap'su•lar
cap'su•late' *also* cap'-
　su•lat'ed
cap'su•la'tion
cap'sule
cap'sul•ize', -ized',
　-iz'ing
cap'tain
cap'tain•cy
cap'tion
cap'tious
cap'ti•vate', -vat'ed,
　-vat'ing
cap'ti•va'tion
cap'ti•va'tor
cap'tive
cap•tiv'i•ty
cap'tor
cap'ture, -tured, -tur-
　ing
cap'u•chin
cap'y•ba'ra
car

car'a•cal'
car'a•cole' *also* car'-
　a•col'
ca•rafe'
car'a•mel
car'a•mel•ize',
　-ized', -iz'ing
car'a•pace'
car'at *(weight)*
　♦caret, carrot
car'a•van'
car'a•van'sa•ry *also*
　car'a•van'se•rai'
car'a•vel'
car'a•way'
car'bide'
car'bine'
car'bo•hy'drate'
car'bo•lat'ed
car•bol'ic acid
car'bon
car'bo•na'ceous
car'bon•ate', -at'ed,
　-at'ing
car'bon•a'tion
car'bon•a'tor
car•bon'ic acid
car'bon•if'er•ous
　(of carbon)
Car'bon•if'er•ous
　(geologic period)
car'bon•i•za'tion
car'bon•ize', -ized',
　-iz'ing
car'bon•yl'
Car'bo•run'dum®
car•box'yl

car'box•yl'ic
car'boy'
car•bun'cle
car•bun'cu•lar
car'bu•re'tor
car'cass
car•cin'o•gen
car'cin•o•gen'ic
car'ci•no'ma *pl.*
　-mas *or* -ma•ta
car'da•mom *or* car'-
　da•mum, *also* car'-
　da•mon
card'board'
card'hold'er
car'di•ac'
car'di•gan
car'di•nal
car'di•nal•ate
car'di•o•gram'
car'di•o•graph'
car'di•ol'o•gist
car'di•ol'o•gy
car'di•o•pul'mon-
　ar'y
car'di•o•vas'cu•lar
card'sharp' *also* card'-
　sharp'er
care, cared, car'ing
ca•reen' *(to tilt,
　swerve)*
ca•reer' *(life work)*
ca•reer' *(to rush
　headlong)*
care'free'
care'ful
care'giv'er

care'less
ca•ress'
car'et *(proofreading mark)*
  ♦*carat, carrot*
care'tak'er
care'worn'
car'fare'
car'go *pl.* -goes *or* -gos
car'hop'
Car'ib•be'an
car'i•bou' *pl.* -bou' *or* -bous
car'i•ca•ture', -tured', -tur'ing
car'i•ca•tur'ist
car'ies *(decay)*
  ♦*carries*
car'il•lon'
car'i•ous
car'load'
Car'mel•ite'
car'mine
car'nage
car'nal
car•nal'i•ty
car•na'tion
car•nel'ian
car'ni•val
car'ni•vore'
car•niv'o•rous
car'no•tite'
car'ob
car'ol *(to sing)*, -oled *or* -olled, -ol•ing *or* -ol•ling
  ♦*carrel*

Car'o•lin'i•an
car'om
car'o•tene'
ca•rot'e•noid'
ca•rot'id
ca•rous'al *(revelry)*
  ♦*carousel*
ca•rouse', -roused', -rous'ing
car'ou•sel' *(merry-go-round)*, *or* car'rou•sel'
  ♦*carousal*
ca•rous'er
carp *(fish)*, *pl.* carp *or* carps
carp *(to complain)*
car'pal *(of the carpus)*
car'pel *(flower part)*
car'pen•ter
car'pen•try
car'pet
car'pet•bag'
car'pet•bag'ger
car'-pool'
car'-pool'er
car'port'
car'pus *pl.* -pi'
car'rel *(library nook)*
  ♦*carol*
car'riage
car'ri•er
car'ri•on
car'rot *(vegetable)*
  ♦*carat, caret*
car'ry, -ried, -ry•ing
car'ry•all'

car'ry•back'
car'ry-o'ver
car'sick'
cart'age
carte blanche'
car•tel'
car'ti•lage
car'ti•lag'i•nous
car•tog'ra•pher
car•tog'raph'ic *also* car'to•graph'i•cal
car•tog'ra•phy
car'ton
car•toon'
car•toon'ist
car'tridge
cart'wheel'
carve, carved, carv'ing
carv'er
car'y•at'id *pl.* -ids *or* -i•des'
car'y•op'sis *pl.* -ses' *or* -si•des'
ca•sa'ba
Cas'a•no'va
cas•cade', -cad'ed, -cad'ing
cas•car'a
case, cased, cas'ing
case'hard'en
ca'sein'
case'ment
case'work'
case'work'er
cash *(money)*
  ♦*cache*

cash'ew
cash•ier' *(financial officer)*
ca•shier' *(to dismiss)*
cash'mere'
cas'ing
ca•si'no *pl.* -nos
cask
cas'ket
Cas•san'dra
cas•sa'va
cas•se•role'
cas•sette'
cas'sia
cas'sock
cas'sou•let'
cas'so•war'y
cast *(to throw),* cast, cast'ing
♦*caste*
cas'ta•nets'
cast'a•way'
caste *(social class)*
♦*cast*
cas'tel•lat'ed
cast'er *(wheel),* also cas'tor
cas'ti•gate', -gat'ed, -gat'ing
cas'ti•ga'tion
cas'ti•ga'tor
cast'-i'ron *adj.*
cas'tle, -tled, -tling
cast'off' *n.*
cast'-off' *adj.*
cas'tor *(oil)*
♦*caster*

cas'trate', -trat'ed, -trat'ing
cas•tra'tion
cas'u•al
cas'u•al•ty
cas'u•ist
cas'u•is'tic
cas'u•ist•ry
ca'sus bel'li'
cat
cat'a•bol'ic
ca•tab'o•lism
cat'a•clysm
cat'a•clys'mic *also* cat'a•clys'mal
cat'a•combs'
cat'a•falque'
cat'a•lep'sy
cat'a•lep'tic
cat'a•logue', -logued', -logu'ing, *also* cat'a•log', -loged', -log'ing
cat'a•logu'er *also* cat'a•log'er
ca•tal'pa
ca•tal'y•sis *pl.* -ses'
cat'a•lyst
cat'a•lyt'ic
cat'a•lyze', -lyzed', -lyz'ing
cat'a•ma•ran'
cat'a•mount'
cat'a•pult'
cat'a•ract'
ca•tarrh'
ca•tarrh'al *also* ca-

tarrh'ous
ca•tas'tro•phe
cat'a•stroph'ic
ca•tas'tro•phism
cat'a•to'ni•a
cat'a•ton'ic
cat'bird'
cat'boat'
cat'call'
catch, caught, catch'-ing
catch'all'
catch'er
catch'i•ness
catch'word'
catch'y
cat'e•chism
cat'e•chist
cat'e•chi•za'tion
cat'e•chize', -chized', -chiz'ing
cat'e•chu'men
cat'e•gor'i•cal
cat'e•go•ri•za'tion
cat'e•go•rize', -rized', -riz'ing
cat'e•go'ry
cat'e•nate', -nat'ed, -nat'ing
cat'e•na'tion
ca'ter
cat'er-cor'nered *also* cat'er-cor'ner, cat'ty-cor'nered
cat'er•pil'lar
cat'er•waul'
cat'fight'

cat'fish' *pl.* -fish' *or*
   -fish'es
cat'gut'
ca•thar'sis *pl.* -ses'
ca•thar'tic
ca•the'dral
cath'e•ter
cath'ode'
cath'ode-ray' tube
cath'o•lic *(universal)*
Cath'o•lic *(of the
   Catholic Church)*
Ca•thol'i•cism
cath'o•lic'i•ty
cat'i'on
cat'i•on'ic
cat'kin'
cat'like'
cat'nip'
cat'-o'-nine'-tails'
cat's'-eye'
cat's'-paw' *also* cats'-
   paw'
cat'tail'
cat'tle
cat'ty
cat'walk'
Cau•ca'sian
Cau'ca•soid'
cau'cus *pl.* -cus•es *or*
   -cus•ses
cau'cus, -cused *or*
   -cussed, -cus•ing *or*
   -cus•sing
cau'dal
cau'date' *also* cau'-
   dat•ed

cau'li•flow'er
caulk *also* calk
caus'al
cau•sal'i•ty
cau•sa'tion
caus'a•tive
cause, caused, caus'-
   ing
cause cé•lè'bre *pl.*
   causes célè'bres
cause'way'
caus'tic
cau'ter•i•za'tion
cau'ter•ize', -ized',
   -iz'ing
cau'tion
cau'tion•ar'y
cau'tious
cav'al•cade'
cav'a•lier'
cav'al•ry
cave, caved, cav'ing
ca've•at'
cave'-in' *n.*
cav'ern
cav'ern•ous
cav'i•ar' *also* cav'-
   i•are'
cav'il, -iled *or* -illed,
   -il'ing *or* -il'ling
cav'i•ta'tion
cav'i•ty
ca•vort'
caw
cay *(islet)*
   ♦*key, quay*
cay•enne' pepper

Cay•use' *pl.* -use' *or*
   -us'es
cease, ceased, ceas'ing
cease'-fire'
ce'cal
ce•cro'pi•a moth
ce'cum *pl.* -ca, *also*
   cae'cum
ce'dar
cede *(to yield),* ced'ed,
   ced'ing
   ♦*seed*
ce•dil'la
ceil'ing
cel'an•dine'
cel'e•brant
cel'e•brate', -brat'ed,
   -brat'ing
cel'e•bra'tion
cel'e•bra'tor
cel'e•bra•to'ry
ce•leb'ri•ty
ce•ler'i•ty
cel'er•y
ce•les'ta *also* ce•leste'
ce•les'tial
ce'li•ac' *also* coe'li•
   ac'
cel'i•ba•cy
cel'i•bate
cell *(room, unit)*
   ♦*sell*
cel'lar *(storage room)*
   ♦*seller*
cell'block'
cell'ist
cell'mate'

cel'lo *pl.* -los
cel'lo•phane'
cel'lu•lar
cel'lu•loid'
cel'lu•lose'
Cel'si•us
Celt'ic *also* Kelt'ic
ce•ment'
cem'e•ter•y
cen'o•bite'
cen'o•bit'ic *also* cen-
   o•bit'i•cal
cen'o•taph'
cen'o•taph'ic
Ce'no•zo'ic
cen'ser *(vessel)*
cen'sor *(examiner)*
cen•so'ri•al
cen•so'ri•ous
cen'sor•ship'
cen'sur•a•ble
cen'sure, -sured, -sur-
   ing
cen'sus *pl.* -sus•es
cent *(coin)*
   ♦*scent, sent*
cen'taur'
cen'tav'o *pl.* -vos
cen•te•nar'i•an
cen•ten'a•ry
cen•ten'ni•al
cen'ter
cen'ter•board'
cen'ter•fold'
cen'ter•piece'
cen'ti•grade'
cen'ti•gram'

cen'ti•li'ter
cen'time'
cen'ti•me'ter
cen'ti•pede'
cen'tral
cen'tral•ism
cen'tral•ist
cen•tral•is'tic
cen•tral'i•ty
cen•tral•i•za'tion
cen'tral•ize', -ized',
   -iz'ing
cen•trif'u•gal
ccn•trif'u•ga'tion
cen'tri•fuge'
cen'tri•ole'
cen•trip'e•tal
cen'trist
cen'troid'
cen'tro•some'
cen•tu'ri•on
cen'tu•ry
ce•phal'ic
ceph'a•lo•pod'
ce•ram'ic
ce•ram'ist
ce're•al *(grain)*
   ♦*serial*
cer'e•bel'lum *pl.*
   -lums *or* -la
cer'e•bral
cer'e•bro•spi'nal
cer'e•brum *pl.*
   -brums *or* -bra
cere'cloth'
cere'ment
cer'e•mo'ni•al

cer'e•mo'ni•ous
cer'e•mo'ny
ce•rise'
ce'ri•um
cer'met'
cer'tain
cer'tain•ty
cer'ti•fi'a•ble
cer•tif'i•cate', -cat'-
   ed, -cat'ing
cer'ti•fi•ca'tion
cer'ti•fy', -fied', -fy'-
   ing
cer'ti•tude'
ce•ru'le•an
cer'vi•cal
cer'vine'
cer'vix *pl.* -vix•es *or*
   -vi•ces'
ce'si•um *also* cae'si-
   um
ces•sa'tion
ces'sion *(surrender-*
   ing)
   ♦*session*
cess'pool'
ce•ta'ce•an
Cha•blis'
cha'-cha'
chafe, chafed,
   chaf'ing
chaff
chaff'er *(one who*
   teases)
chaf'fer *(to bargain)*
chaf'finch
chaf'ing dish

cha•grin′
chain′-re•act′ v.
chain′-smoke′,
 -smoked′, -smok′ing
chair′man
chair′per′son
chair′wom′an
chaise′ longue′ pl.
 chaise′ longues′ or
 chaises′ longues′
chal′ce•don′ic
chal•ced′o•ny
chal′co•cite′
chal′co•py′rite′
cha•let′
chal′ice
chalk′board′
chalk′y
chal′lenge, -lenged,
 -leng•ing
chal′lenge•a•ble
chal′lenge•er
chal′lis
cham′ber
cham′ber•lain
cham′ber•maid′
cham′bray′
cha•me′leon
cham′fer
cham•ois′ (animal),
 pl. -ois
cham′ois (leather), pl.
 -ois, also cham′my
cham′o•mile′ or
 cam′o•mile′
champ
cham•pagne′ (wine)

cham•paign′ (plain)
cham′pi•on
cham′pi•on•ship′
chance, chanced,
 chanc′ing
chan′cel
chan′cel•ler•y
chan′cel•lor
chan′cer•y
chan′cre
chanc′y
chan′de•lier′
chan′dler
chan′dler•y
change, changed,
 chang′ing
change′a•ble
change′ling
change′o′ver
chan′nel
chan′son
chant′er
chan•teuse′
chan′tey (song), pl.
 -teys, also chant′y,
 shant′y
chan′ti•cleer′
Cha′nu•kah also Ha′-
 nuk•kah, Ha′nu•kah
cha′os′
cha•ot′ic
chap, chapped, chap′-
 ping
chap′ar•ral′
chap′book′
cha•peau′ pl. -peaux′
 or -peaus′

chap′el
chap′er•on also chap′-
 er•one′
chap′lain
chap′let
chaps
chap′ter
char, charred, char′-
 ring
char′a•banc′
char′ac•ter
char′ac•ter•is′tic
char′ac•ter•i•za′-
 tion
char′ac•ter•ize′,
 -ized′, -iz′ing
cha•rades′
char′coal′
chard (beet)
 ♦shard
char′don•nay′ or
 Char′don•nay′ pl.
 -nays
charge, charged,
 charg′ing
charge′a•ble
char•gé′ d′af•faires
 pl. char•gés′ d′af-
 faires′
charg′er
char′i•ly
char′i•ness
char′i•ot
char′i•o•teer′
cha•ris′ma
char′is•mat′ic
char′i•ta•ble

char′i•ty
char′la•tan
char′ley horse
char′lotte
charm′er
char•meuse′
char′nel
chart
char′ter
char•treuse′
char′wom′an
char′y
chase, chased, chas′-
　ing
chas′er
chasm
chas′mal
Chas′sid *pl.* -si′dim,
　also Has′sid, Ha′sid
chas′sis *pl.* -sis
chaste *(pure)*, chast′er,
　chast′est
　♦*chased*
chas′ten
chas•tise′, -tised′,
　-tis′ing
chas′ti•ty
chas′u•ble
chat, chat′ted, chat′-
　ting
cha•teau′ *pl.* -teaux′,
　also châ•teau′
chat′e•laine′
chat′tel
chat′ter
chat′ter•box′
chat′ty

chauf′feur
chau′vin•ism
chau′vin•ist
chau′vin•is′tic
cheap *(inexpensive)*
　♦*cheep*
cheap′en
cheap′jack′
cheap′skate′
cheat′er
check *(halt, restraint,*
　verification, bank or-
　der, pattern)
　♦*Czech*
check′a•ble
check′book′
check′er
check′er•board′
check′ered
check′ers
check′mate′, -mat′ed,
　-mat′ing
check′-out′ *n.*
check′point′
check′room′
check′up′ *n.*
Ched′dar *also* ched′-
　dar
cheek′bone′
cheek′y
cheep *(chirp)*
　♦*cheap*
cheer′ful
cheer′lead′er
cheer′y
cheese′burg′er
cheese′cake′

cheese′cloth′
chees′y
chee′tah
chef-d′oeu′vre *pl.*
　chefs-d′oeu′vre
chef′s salad
chem′i•cal
Chemical Mace®
chem′i•lu′mi•nes′-
　cence
che•mise′
chem′ist
chem′is•try
che′mo•syn′the•sis
che′mo•syn•thet′ic
che′mo•tax•on′-
　o•my
che′mo•ther′a•py
chem•ur′gic *also*
　chem•ur′gi•cal
chem•ur•gy
che•nille′
cher′ish
che•root′
cher′ry
cher′ry•stone′
cher′ub *pl.* -u•bim′
che•ru′bic
cher′vil
chesh′ire cheese
chess′board′
chess′man′
chest
ches′ter•field′
chest′nut′
chev′a•lier′
chev′i•ot

chev'ron
chew'ing gum
che•wink'
chew'y
Chi•an'ti
chi•a'ro•scu'ro pl.
-ros
chic (stylish)
♦chick, sheik
Chi•ca'na
chi•can'er•y
Chi•ca'no pl. -nos
chick (young bird)
♦chic
chick'a•dee'
chick'en
chick'en-heart'ed
chick'en-liv'ered
chick'pea'
chick'weed'
chic'le
chic'o•ry
chide, chid'ed or chid,
chid'ed or chid or
chid'den, chid'ing
chief 'ly
chief 'tain
chif•fon'
chif 'fo•nier'
chig'ger
chi•gnon'
Chi•hua'hua
chil'blain'
child pl. chil'dren
child'bear'ing
child'birth'
child'hood'

child'ish
child'like'
Chil'e•an
chil'e con car'ne
also chil'i con car'ne
chil'i (pepper), pl. -ies,
also chil'e, chil'li pl.
-lies
chill'y (cold)
♦chili
chime, chimed, chim'-
ing
chim'er
chi•me'ra
chi•mer'i•cal
chim'i•chan'ga
chim'ney pl. -neys
chimp
chim'pan•zee'
chin, chinned, chin'-
ning
chi'na
chi'na•ber'ry
Chi'na•town'
chi'na•ware'
chinch
chin•chil'la
chine
Chi•nese' pl. -nese'
chink
chi'no pl. -nos
chi•nook'
chin'qua•pin'
chintz'y
chip, chipped, chip'-
ping
chip'munk'

Chip'pen•dale'
chip'per
chi'ro•man'cy
chi•rop'o•dist
chi•rop'o•dy
chi'ro•prac'tic
chi'ro•prac'tor
chirp'er
chirr (trill)
♦churr
chir'rup
chis'el, -eled or -elled,
-el•ing or -el•ling
chi'-square'
chit'chat', -chat'ted,
-chat'ting
chi'tin (hornlike sub-
stance)
chi'ton (mollusk)
chit'ter
chit'ter•lings also
chit'lins, chit'lings
chi•val'ric
chiv'al•rous
chiv'al•ry
chive
chlo'ral
chlo'rate'
chlor'dane' also
chlor'dan'
chlo'ride'
chlo'rin•ate', -at'ed,
-at'ing
chlo'rine'
chlo'rite'
chlo'ro•form'
chlo'ro•phyll also